CROSSING BORDERS

BY MICHAEL FERRIS

"Crossing Borders," by Michael Ferris. ISBN 978-1-60264-373-4.

Published 2009 by Virtualbookworm.com Publishing Inc., P.O. Box 9949, College Station, TX 77842, US. ©2009, Michael Ferris. All rights reserved.

Manufactured in the United States of America.

TAKING OFF

After high school, I was a typical small-town red-blooded American boy in Michigan, working for my father who had a small music store located in Benton Harbor. The store sold all types of musical instruments to all walks of life. My mother's beauty salon was just a hop, skip, and a jump away, right down the road from him. Up until that point, I had never left the United States and to be honest with you, never really been out of my own city that much. A big trip for me would have been driving with my parents an hour away to South Bend, Indiana, or Kalamazoo, Michigan. Chicago was two and half hours away and even going there was like making a trip around the world. Now, it was time for me to literally make a trip half way across the planet and I wasn't even sure when and if I was coming back.

"Bye Grandma! Bye Dad!" saying farewell to them both as I was getting ready to leave. They had just driven three hours to O'Hare International Airport in Chicago to see me off. It was my first trip alone and the first time I had ever set foot on a plane. Giving them one last glance, I took my guitar, and literally ran through the gate so that I wouldn't have time to be afraid of leaving.

———————

Having found my seat, I started clutching the ring my father had given me at breakfast that morning to bring luck. It was the gold ring he had always worn since I was a child and it meant quite a bit that he would present me with something that meant so much to him. As a small boy I remember seeing it near his bed while he slept. Now it was on my finger while leaving the country. I was on my way to Vienna, Austria, a city known throughout the decades for its classical music, located in the heart of Europe. For the entire past year, I had been counting down the days until my flight and couldn't wait. Finally, the day of my departure had arrived. Thinking about the fact that my waiting had come to an end, never having left my own city before on my own, I was scared to death.

Suddenly, fear set in and I started having second thoughts about the whole thing. A craziness took hold of me and I got up from my seat, ran to the stewardess and said, "I changed my mind! Please, could you let me off?"

"No, Sir, we have already shut the door for departure. I do apologize, but at this time, we can't let anyone off the plane," she said, as she looked at me a bit confounded.

Returning to my seat, I started clutching the

ring again. Even though I was afraid, there was part of me that was happy that the door was shut, not allowing me to change my mind. After all, I had been practicing the guitar so much and it seemed so obvious that nothing could stop me from passing that entrance exam at the Viennese Academy of Music. A new chapter in my life was soon to begin.

In the seat right next to me, there was an older lady who was drinking a McDonald's milkshake. I could see that it was chocolate because it was all over her face. As the plane started picking up pace, she put the empty cup into the netting on the back of the seat in front of her. When we took off, the cup slipped out of the netting onto the floor. Surprisingly enough, it hadn't been empty and the chocolate goo spilled everywhere, splattering onto my blue jeans. I was absolutely furious. The thought of having to take my first flight all full of chocolate and arriving to Vienna with a huge stain covering my pants completely frustrated me.

As the stewardess passed, she looked at the mess all over the floor. Glancing toward the old lady, she asked her if she was all right. Then, her eyes raced into my direction with what seemed to be a look of disgust. It didn't take much to realize that she had accused me of spilling the milk, instead of giving the blame to my innocent-looking neighbor. After asking her for help to clean up the mess, the stewardess came and gave me some newspapers to put over the puddle on the floor. For eight entire hours, I had to sit and endure the smell of wet chocolate. My hands could not help but to touch my blue jeans again and again to see if the stickiness had gone away after trying to wash it off. I couldn't help getting red in the face with rage.

After arriving, getting my luggage, and finding the train into the city, I boarded and took a seat across from two sweet little ladies that must have been in their late sixties or early seventies. It was pretty exciting to try out my foreign language abilities for the first time with real native speakers. I said hello to them in German and they retorted by asking me where I was from. I had only been learning German for the past year at a local college so I could communicate, but that was all.

Whenever I said something to the ladies, they seemed to understand the point I was trying to get across, but I was having great difficulty understanding anything they were saying. The only thing I could make out was the German word for yes. Instead of admitting to my inability to speak the language, I just pretended to understand, nodding my head again and again.

That turned out to be quite a problem when they asked me why my pants were full of sticky chocolate. I just stared at them with a dazed look nodding while saying, "Yes, I understand."

As the conductor came checking tickets, he started yelling at the group of people sitting nearby on account of the fact that they had their feet propped up against the seat across from them. Obviously, it was not allowed to put your feet up on the train seats, which I figured by singling out the word "*Fuss*" in his monologue. My fellow travelers turned out to be Americans also, who repeatedly told the conductor, "We don't speak German."

I was just getting ready to enter into the conversation and impress them with my interpreting skills when the conductor started hitting their feet violently and yelling. Witnessing this act, I realized that he didn't need an interpreter. My fellow patriots got the point quite quickly. Without a doubt, some languages are international. I was just baffled and wondered if something similar would happen in the US without somebody getting sued.

Focusing on my own thoughts again, I started looking out of the window, which was like looking into another world. It wasn't just the language that made me feel far away from home, but the way the light fell on the strange looking buildings, the look on everyone's faces when they talked, lacking a smile, and above all the smell.

Yes, there was an odor in the air since I had arrived. In addition to the smell, it occurred to me how colorful everything was. There were so many buildings that were painted in pastel colors. I found it absolutely beautiful. Having read it in my guide book, I was aware that Vienna was a big city. Smiling at the older ladies sitting across from me, I said in my very best German, "This city is big!"

They both chattered something back that made me think of the possibility that they were speaking another language all together. Unfortunately, I heard the word, "*Ja*," confirming that they were truly speaking German. This was also my own personal verification of how much more I would have to learn if I wanted to stay there.

After a few moments, I then said in my very best German. "This city is beautiful!" gazing at all of the huge ornate stone houses with beautiful cast iron balconies full of flowers as our train passed. The two older ladies both answered me with an avalanche of words and I nodded back with a mere smile.

"*Bist du alleine hier?*" asked the ladies, wanting to know if I was traveling by myself. I was aware that I looked a lot younger than my age. Trying to calm them by saying how old I was, the concerned look on their faces did not disappear. I am not sure to this day if it was my age or my German skills that made them worry so much.

"I have to buy a ticket for the subway," asking them if they knew where the nearest ticket agent was when I got off the train. By the look on their faces, it was apparent that they had not only understood exactly what I had said, but also knew exactly where to buy a ticket. Unfortunately, I still didn't.

As I was exiting the train and started walking toward the entrance hall of the station, the two elderly ladies were waiting for me anxiously. They were trying to say something with no avail and ended up taking me by the arm and literally leading me like a blind man to a tobacco shop where they actually purchased a subway ticket for me with their own money. While entering, I gazed around and realized that the little tobacco shop did not only sell cigarettes but also magazines, postcards, and what seemed to be lottery tickets. As they were opening the door, the ladies made gestures for me to follow them, which at the time, seemed a bit scary.

Trying to convey that it wasn't necessary that they accompany me any further, I took out the piece of notebook paper that my guitar teacher, who had lived in Vienna for a long time, had given me. In my eyes, this was the proof that I knew where to go. He had written exact instructions on how to get to the church he had arranged for me to stay at.

After careful examination, the older ladies took me by the arm again, leading me right down into the subway where they put me on and said goodbye. As the subway doors were closing, I finally understood something they were saying. *"Auf Wiedersehen!"* Vienna had given me quite a warm welcome.

The instructions that I had been given to find the church were really very helpful and unimaginably detailed. *"Get off subway, turn right, go down steps, take tram thirty-one."* On the subway and on the tram, I kept hearing the names of the stops in German being called out on the loud speaker. Although it was really difficult to make them out, I somehow managed to arrive at the church in no time at all. Upon arrival, I could not get the thought out of my head that I had actually made it. The two ladies from the train would have been so proud of me!

Finally walking into the church, a group of people were rehearsing on a piano and singing. I stood for a few minutes at the entrance and admired them and my new surroundings with awe. As the music continued, I noticed that the church was very plain with high ceilings and many wooden fixtures on the walls. All of the doors had huge metal handles on them. The windows were also very odd. They seemed to open from the top, tilted inward, as if they were ready to fall out of the wall. Suddenly, the group stopped in the middle of the song they were singing and looked at me, asking me if they could help me in some way. After realizing that I hadn't understood, they asked again, this time in English.

To my dismay, no one knew anything about me staying there. Feeling a bit out of place, I explained to them that arrangements had been made for me to spend the night at the church. Looking at me a bit confounded, they told me that it was necessary to wait and ask Herr Fuchsel, the church director.

After about an hour, an old man finally came and introduced himself as the person I had been waiting for. At that point, my head started feeling really dizzy due to being so tired from the flight and the horrendous time change of six hours. Reading about jet lag is a lot different than really having it. Meeting Herr Fuchsel was not a very pleasant experience at all. After taking me to the room I was to spend the night in, he felt it was necessary to share his opinion of the American people. It was the first time I had ever heard anyone talk about Americans like that in my life, yet it was also my first time abroad.

"I know how wasteful Americans are!" impressing upon me not to keep the lights on for very long or use very much water. Unfortunately for me, Herr Fuchsel was one of the first people that spoke English very well. If I hadn't met the older ladies earlier in the train, my impression of the country would have been quite a bit different.

After explaining an array of rules to be obeyed, he asked me where my sleeping bag was. "What? Why don't you have a sleeping bag?" he asked. "You must go and buy one! You can't sleep on the bed without a sleeping bag, you will make it dirty." He gave me keys to the church and left me alone, imploring me to find a sleeping bag before sleeping on the bed. At that moment, I could have very easily just passed out asleep. Looking at the bed and thinking about all the things that had just been said to me, in spite of my weariness caused by sleep deprivation due to the excitement, it had become my mission to go out and find a sleeping bag.

I exited the church and started walking around in search of a sports-goods store. For some reason, maybe due to jet lag and me being so tired, it didn't occur to me exactly where the church was located, nor the fact that the probability of finding a sleeping bag in a city suburb wasn't very high. I ended up getting completely lost.

I kept asking people on the street where there might be a store, but they answered me back in German, which I barely understood. After about two hours of walking in circles, I finally found my way back to the church, empty handed. Balling up my fists and almost pouting, I hurried back to my room, lay on the floor, and cried myself to sleep.

I was awoken by a young man opening the door. He seemed to be about my age. "What are you doing on the floor?" he asked with an accent which sounded like a younger version of Herr Fuchsel's. Although, I have to admit that his English had surpassed my German by leaps and bounds.

"I don't have a sleeping bag," I said, "and Herr Fuchsel said that I have to have one in order to sleep on the bed."

"Ah yes, you must have a sleeping bag, or you will make the bed dirty. I will ask my mother if she has one for you," he said, leaving the room after briskly taking a few papers from the table.

I just couldn't understand why the sleeping bag had been so important, but this young man was obviously my only chance of getting one. I kept thinking to myself, *"Otherwise, I may have to sleep on the floor for a whole week."*

Erik, who turned out to be one of my first good friends in Austria, ended up coming later with a red sleeping bag. It was as if my prayers had been answered. Erik was accompanied by a young woman, who presented me with a big bowl of fruit, full of apples, bananas, oranges and pears. Both of them were musicians. To my surprise, they brought out their guitars at that very instant and started singing and playing songs, which cheered me up to a great extent.

Although the atmosphere was still very foreign to me, for the first time since I had arrived,

I finally relaxed a little and started enjoying being half way across the world. I was in the land of music at last. Listening to my new friends singing, looking at my bowl of fruit, and holding that red sleeping bag, I couldn't have been happier. That moment seemed so magical that I will never forget it for as long as I live. This was my first day in Austria.

THE PRATER, THE BEAR AND THE BILINGUAL PIMP

A couple of days later, I was sitting in a go-go bar, holding a huge teddy bear in my arms.

The purpose of my trip to Vienna had to do with hopes of being able to study classical guitar there, but unfortunately, I hadn't passed the entrance exam. Sitting in that bar was just a small part of one of the most disappointing days I had ever had. I was about to go home a failure, but had three more days before my returning flight to the United States. Then, it occurred to me that I was in Europe. *"I should just make a vacation out of this whole disaster,"* I said to myself.

After pondering for a while, I decided to go to the Prater, an amusement park located in the northeastern part of the city. I wanted to go there because it was supposed to have one of the biggest and oldest Ferris wheels in the whole world.

For some strange reason, being alone in Vienna made me get lost in my own thoughts as I traveled using the city's wonderful transportation system including street trams, buses, and an underground subway. It could have been because everything was such a new experience; maybe, it was because the people were so different. Seeing that I had been so depressed due to the music school not accepting me, I was completely lost in thought while reading my guide book.

I thought about the fact that Austria had once been a monarchy under the rule of an emperor. The country had been a major power in Europe until the end of WWI, after which it was forced to become a very small country. Not too long afterwards, it was annexed to Nazi Germany during the time of Hitler.

Before becoming the cruel dictator he was, Hitler actually came to Vienna to become an artist. He didn't pass the entrance exam for the art school he wanted to get into and started painting postcards for a living.

Years later, after taking control of Germany, he came back to the city, this time marching in with an army. While giving his speech, thousands of Viennese inhabitants cheered him on. After Hitler's defeat, Vienna was split up between the allied forces and had been occupied for quite a while by the French, the Russians, the British, and the United States. Austria is now a neutral country and home to the United Nations. To make a long story short, all of these things contributed to my thinking that Vienna was a very peculiar city and I closed the book.

On my way to the Prater, looking at the huge Ferris wheel in the distance, I walked through this big open park with a lot of homeless and all kinds of other people whose presence you wouldn't normally go looking for. A beggar approached asking me for money. Giving him like twenty dollars worth in Austrian money didn't really seemed to matter as I took the bill out of my pocket and handed it to him. My dreams of being a guitarist in Vienna had been ruined and nothing seemed to matter anymore.

"NO! You can't give me that much!" he yelled, trying to give the money back to me. It was quite surprising why he wouldn't have taken it without saying a word. I learned later that this was not the Austrian way of thinking. To give a beggar money is good, but to give him too much, in the eyes of an Austrian, is absurd. Even for the beggar, it was absolutely unacceptable.

"It doesn't matter. Have fun with it," I said, thinking of how worthless money was after such a huge disappointment. The man finally thanked me and went on his merry way, shaking his head in disbelief as he turned away from me.

Arriving at the Prater was a really beautiful sight. The whole area was just enormous. There were rides and games everywhere, coffee shops, bars, and even a carousel for children with real horses!

I started thinking about the fact that the drinking age in Austria was only sixteen, wondering if I could really buy alcohol. I went to the next outdoor café and asked the waiter if I could have a glass of wine, being quite nervous doing so. I thought he would ask me my age. On the contrary, he said, "Would you like red or white?"

"A red wine, please," I answered. The wine made me feel better, although I still felt like a failure. I kept looking up at the beautiful sunny blue sky and kept wondering what I was doing there. Glancing around at all of the rides and fairground music going on, I just wanted to go home.

At that moment, a man at a stand started yelling something in German, trying to get my attention. He was holding an air gun.

"It's time to forget about the school and have a little bit of fun," I thought.

"How much does it cost to play?" I asked him.

"No English, No English," he said. It was time to try out my German again. He told me it cost fourteen shillings a shot. The goal was to hit the target five times in order to win a gigantic teddy bear. I don't think I mentioned that fourteen Austrian schillings were worth one dollar at the time. After trying to shoot at the target several times, I asked how much money I was up to. Looking at the figure typed into the calculator almost made me faint. What I wasn't aware of was the subtle difference in German between the numbers fourteen and forty (namely *vierzehn* and *vierzig*). It cost forty shillings per shot and not fourteen as I had thought. My bill was already up to several hundred shillings adding up to around sixty US dollars. Oh gosh was that a nightmare!

Debating if I should make a run for it, I started looking around and spotted a police officer. The police officer was dressed differently than in the US, but it wasn't difficult to recognize someone wearing a uniform and a gun in public. I kept alternating my gaze from the police officer to the calculator and then back again. Then I thought about the entrance exam that afternoon and decided to take a few more shots at the target.

In the end, I had goose bumps because I was so excited. Taking that teddy bear off the hook made me feel like I had achieved something at last. It only cost me eighty dollars. It was the biggest teddy bear I had ever seen. It just felt grand to have won such a prize. That bear, strangely enough, was exactly what I needed to lift my spirits.

Along with the rides, games, and carousel with real horses, was something else that would interest any other eighteen-year-old American boy alone in Europe. In the middle of this beautiful park, there was a go-go strip bar and, in Europe, I was old enough to get in.

Entering and taking a seat, it wasn't just the naked lady that was so amusing for me. It was the whole atmosphere of being in a real European bar. Everybody was drinking wine and smoking cigarettes and they all had a very exotic European air. These people had an "*I go to a go-go bar everyday*" look about them, which in my eighteen-year-old eyes was really interesting and very mature.

At the little table I was sitting at, I just

couldn't get over the fact that they were all looking at me. Was I imagining it? Even the dancer seemed to be watching me! This persisted until it occurred to me that they were not looking at me at all. Their point of interest was not even the naked lady; it was the enormous teddy bear sitting on the chair next to me.

After realizing what was going on, I noticed that the bartender was trying to encourage me to give the bear to the dancer, who by that time was already dancing around my table. I didn't want to give up my prize.

———————

Leaving the bar quite embarrassed and walking back through the park, the beggar I had given the money to came up from behind wanting to shake my hand and thank me once again. It actually scared the living daylights out of me at first, yet the man was harmless, he just wanted to show me how much he appreciated the money, which actually made me feel a little better.

I took the street tram back to the church I was staying at. Everyone was staring at me. A man on the tram who spoke English quite well kept talking to me, asking me where I had got the bear and where I was from. He spoke English perfectly and didn't have a German accent at all, which at the time, struck me as odd. Whispering into my ear, he started asking me if I liked the girl sitting across from us, who seemed to be about fourteen years of age.

"Do you like this girl?" he said, "because she likes you very much."

"What do you mean?" I asked a bit confused. There were so many thoughts going on in my head, out of fear and disgust, it took me a few seconds to realize that he was trying to sell me a child prostitute. I don't know exactly what I was thinking at that very moment. *Was it the money I had lost? The embarrassment I had at the bar? Or even the sickness of a bi-lingual pimp selling children?*

Realizing the answer (thinking about going home to the US and to my family and friends a failure), I immediately exited the tram at the next stop and waited for another one to come. In my mind, I was about to scream out, "*Why me?!*" and I clutched that teddy bear with all my might. God, I loved that bear!

GETTING SETTLED IN A MOUNTAIN VILLAGE

G etting off the bus in the village high up on the mountain and walking a while, I gazed at the mountain range surrounding me and thought, *"I would have never guessed that a place like this existed. It is so gorgeous!"* The houses surrounding me were very strange looking. They all looked like barn houses, made of wood with masses of colorful flowers all over their windows. It also struck me as odd that there was a strange odor of cow manure in the air. After walking for a while holding my nose, it occurred to me there were no telephones anywhere and that the whole area was completely empty. There were no people, just these barns everywhere and the smell of cows.

The only thing I had was an address on a piece of paper with the instructions, *"Get off the bus and turn to your right."* After about fifteen minutes of walking, a woman with white hair and big glasses came out and greeted me in German, asking me to follow her. My German was getting better and better since my trip to Vienna four months ago, but I was still having some difficulties understanding the language. Although I could barely make out what she was saying, I could tell without a doubt that this was the lady I was supposed to talk to about renting a room. Following her, she took me straight to her house. It was similar to all the other barn-like houses in the village, but seemed quite a bit bigger.

She showed me a room on the second floor. Being only nineteen, I had never had to look for an apartment or do anything similar before in my whole life, much less in a foreign country. To be quite honest, I wouldn't have even known where to start looking if I had had to do it all on my own. For this reason, it was great that the viewing of this room had been arranged for me. The room consisted of a bed, a desk, and a little separate bathroom with a small shower and a sliding wooden door. It was very simple and not very welcoming, but on the other hand, it would be a place to stay. "I'll take it," I told my new landlady.

The lady's daughter appeared, coming to assist her mother. She spoke a bit of English with me, explaining how much the room cost and the rules of the house. The lady only leased a few of her many rooms to students in need. The other rooms were reserved for the guests of this bed and breakfast hotel who wanted to spend their holidays in that little village named Birgitz, located just outside of Innsbruck, Austria, right in the middle of the mountains.

The rules of the house were very strict. It was the second time I had been confronted with

Austrians being so frugal. Several things were made quite clear to me. The lights were always to be turned off if I wasn't using them. I was also told about wasting water and that showering for more than a few minutes was forbidden. For this reason, instructions on how to shower were explained to me in great detail. I was to wet down my body, turn off the water, use soap and then rinse, turning off the water immediately after the soap had been washed away from my skin. It was all a bit stressful at first, but I thought, *"When in Rome, do as the Romans do."* After all the rules had been thoroughly introduced, I was left all alone to sit in what was to be my new home. As I peered out of my window, the view of the mountains with their peaks piercing into the clouds was almost shocking. *"Am I in a dream?"*

My thoughts started wandering back to how I had failed the entrance exam in Vienna and what a huge disappointment it had been for me. And now, only four months later, I found myself sitting in a small room in Birgitz, alone, not knowing what to do.

———————

The voice of the lady telling me that I had just passed the entrance exam at the Mozarteum University in Salzburg was echoing in my mind. It made me smile for the mere reason that I knew for sure that my goal to study the guitar in Austria had become reality.

The teacher who had taken me on as a student

accepted me on the sole condition that I move to Innsbruck, the city where she was living. There was a branch of the main school there where I could take a lot of my courses and have guitar lessons with her once or twice a week. She had arranged for me to take a look at this room. Somehow, one of her students had let her know that there had been a room available. That is how I ended up living right in the middle of a mountain range known as the Alps.

Once again, I was really tired and exhausted. The smell since I had entered the house was very evident in my new little room. Contrary to the smell of manure outside, it was a very moist and clean odor, but at the same time, it reminded me of the smell of an old basement. As I opened the window, the vague smell of manure and mountain air rushed into the room. Suddenly having to hold my nose, I almost involuntarily slammed the window shut again. Throughout my future travels, I have realized that every single place on this Earth has a distinct odor. It is an interesting phenomenon. For sure, there is no place in the world that smells just like Birgitz. Staring out of the window, I was again awed by the silvery mountain peaks that seemed to go on into infinity. It was just amazing!

I started thinking of what to do next. *"Should I sleep or just sit here?"* I thought. *"Jet lag must be getting to me again."*

Seeing that the new landlady told me there were two other students living with me in the hotel, I decided to go exploring my new home and seek them out. As I walked through the long hallways, the fact that everything was made of rustic wood really impressed me. The carpentry was so beautiful; it was as if the entire house had been constructed for the filming of a fairy tale. The furniture all around was ornately carved out of oak and laminated. The doors even matched the furniture and were cut out in the same design. The gigantic door handles were made of shiny brass and almost seemed to glow as they reflected the sunlight coming through the windows.

I knocked on the door of the person the landlady had pointed out as being the student, who also studied under my new guitar teacher. He had actually arranged for me to view the room, so I decided to thank him. I heard footsteps and the door opened. The young man standing in front of me asked me in German, then in English, "What do you want?"

"Hi, I am Michael and I just moved in. I heard we have the same teacher at university," I said.

"Ah, you. My name is Roman. Would you like some coffee?" he asked without replying to what I had said. I accepted the invitation and he led me in to his room and gave me a hot cup of coffee. It was so strong I thought I couldn't drink it.

"Wow, that is some strong coffee," I said.

"What? It is good coffee, I just bought it yesterday," he answered. This was my first encounter with European coffee, which is so strong that drinking more than a single cup would probably amount to the level of caffeine in a strong pot of coffee in the United States. "You drink your coffee very weak in America, don't you?" he asked, "I read in a book that American coffee is supposed to be like dirty water. This is a real coffee."

"Well, until now, I never thought coffee in the United States was weak. But compared to this, it surely is," I said.

After finishing, without a moment's notice, he asked me, "Are you hungry? If you want, you can eat with me. I am making chicken."

Due to all the excitement of moving to Innsbruck and getting accepted by the school, I forgot to eat anything the whole day. Then, it occurred to me that I would not have known where to get any food, even if I wanted to. It was a mountain village and it wasn't even clear if there was a supermarket nearby. I had to admit that I was starving. "Thanks, if you don't mind, I would love some chicken," I said without hesitating, even though the invitation seemed a bit out of the blue.

Roman took me to the kitchen where he started cooking. He explained to me how important it was to clean the kitchen because the landlady did not want to ever come in and see a dirty kitchen. She threatened that if she did, we would lose our privileges to cook in her kitchen, which for a student on a budget could be detrimental.

As I sat there, I asked Roman, "So where are you from?" There was no answer. I kept asking, "Where are you from?" thinking that he could not understand my English.

"It is not so important where I am from," he said.

I decided to let the topic drop and not anger the person that had just invited me to dinner without even knowing me. I started looking at the canned goods standing around in the kitchen and asked him out of curiosity for the language, "How do you say the word 'peach' in German?" and asked, "Do you like peaches? I don't like them very much."

Suddenly, he looked at me aghast as if I had asked him something horribly insulting.

"Why did you ask that?!?! Why you ask that!?" he repeated again and again, horrified at my innocent question. I didn't know how to react and just let it drop, giving him a grimace conveying to him that there must have been a misunderstanding. But, the way he yelled at me, I was having serious thoughts about sharing his dinner.

Despite this incident and the confusion, Roman ended up becoming one of my best pals in Innsbruck and remains a friend to this very day.

It was not until a long time afterwards that I finally found out why Roman had invited me to dinner. As a student, financial means are not exactly coming out of your ears, so it was really kind of him to invite me to share half of his dinner.

Sitting on the wooden chair of his room several months later, he told me what he thought of me the first day we had met.

"Michael, you looked absolutely horrible and I thought you were starving. You were the first American I had ever met personally and I have to admit, you weren't what I was expecting from the richest country in the world. You looked really hungry and exhausted!"

"I had a long day behind me," I exclaimed, a bit red in the face and once again I thought about the fact that abroad, even a single person can sometimes get into the sticky situation of unknowingly being representative of an entire country. This always made me feel quite uneasy and still does to this very day. Nevertheless, for me, Roman has always represented the Czech Republic, his fatherland. It wasn't until he got to know me better that he told me about his Czech origins.

At first, thinking that an American would have had something against someone from "Eastern Europe", he didn't want to tell me where he was from. It was quite surprising to him that it didn't matter to me whatsoever. In fact, I thought it was great to meet someone from the Czech Republic. Coming to Austria, I had only thought about meeting other Austrians. Meeting someone from a completely different country seemed more exciting than ever.

Only later did I find out that there are a lot of people from the Eastern European countries living in Austria. They are quite often confronted with prejudices, similar to the racist issue against migrant workers in the United States. Due to the kindness Roman showed me that day, it is something I have never understood.

Later on that year, a few weeks before Roman came with me to the US to visit my family, I even found out why he reacted the way he did when I asked him about the German word for '*peach*' that day. The word '*peach*' in Czech is a very bad word for female genitalia; in fact, it is the worst term in the whole language. In his eyes, I had been interrogating him for several minutes, inquiring about the dirtiest word he was aware of. Roman was just shocked, even sickened, that I wanted to know this right before eating dinner and was even more surprised when I finally explained that, in English, it was just a harmless piece of fruit. This story taught me that when abroad, you always have to be careful of what you say, or at least expect that what you say might be misunderstood.

LOVE AND TROUBLE

Do you remember falling in love for the first time? I think everybody does.

———————

The girl next door to me was just about the most beautiful girl I had ever seen. It wasn't just that though. She was a mixture of everything exotic, everything that was unusual and interesting about being in Europe, not to mention the fact that she actually came from the city my mother had always read to me about, the capital of the old world my grandmother had constantly mentioned, the center of the Roman Empire, the city of the Colosseum, Rome.

She and I did everything together; we went shopping together, walking together and we used to spend hours in her room listening to music. She always told me about how beautiful it was to live in Italy and how she grew up. She was very proud of coming from Rome. As she talked, I discovered my weakness for her gorgeous Italian accent and could listen to her for hours.

Every morning, she would knock on my door to have breakfast and we would make our way to the German course we took together at university.

Afterwards, we went to the library together to write emails to our parents. I could always confide in her when we talked about being homesick. She had the same problem and missed her family very much. Living abroad is probably the most exciting experience on Earth, but it is also quite a sacrifice to be away from your family for such a long period of time. I was eight hours away by plane, while she was eight hours away by train. We were both far away from home and wished that our families could come and visit us more often.

Only being nineteen years old, I wanted to spend my whole future with her. Along with German, I even started learning Italian on my own, thinking it would bring us closer. *Amore*. This is the first word that I learned in Italian, because I was in love with a beautiful long-haired Italian girl.

If it hadn't been for her boyfriend, this might have even worked. In a nutshell, instead of becoming wild lovers, I became her best friend. It was my own fault that I had always had such difficulty telling her how I felt, in fear of losing her friendship. Every kiss that she gave that other man in my presence was like pure torture. *Amore*.

Then it finally happened. After breaking up with her boyfriend, she came to my room that day and asked, "Hi Mike, would you like to go out drinking with me tonight?"

Without even hesitating, "Of course! What time?" I asked.

After arranging to meet her at nine o'clock, I thought my dreams had come true. That night however, I found out how much beer my true love could drink. Liter after liter of beer. Still, I enjoyed being with her so much that it didn't bother me. *Amore*.

At the bar where we went to, we met a group of her friends. What a fabulous evening until it was time to leave. By the time we started thinking about going home, it was about three o'clock in the morning. Along with the winter snow, it was very cold outside. There would not be any buses back to our little village until much later that morning.

A friend invited us both to stay at his apartment. At the time, we didn't know what else to do. A taxi back to the little village on the mountain would have cost a fortune. As always, our funds were a bit on the low side.

"He is a good friend," she said. "We can trust him."

We went to his apartment. As he had promised, there was a type of bunk bed to sleep in. I climbed up to the top bed and waited. The girl of my dreams had got a bit ill on account of drinking and was in the bathroom vomiting. After waiting for about ten more minutes and her not coming to our bunk bed, I started getting very worried. As the guy came to bring sheets for the bed, I asked, "So, where is she? Is she okay?"

"*Ich weiss nicht*," saying that he did not know

in German. That answer struck me as being a bit odd.

A few minutes later, I started hearing strange noises coming from the room next to me. The bunk bed was right up against the wall. Several minutes had passed before realizing what the sounds were. The both of them were in the room right next to me having sex. I kept thinking how much both of them had just drunk and was hoping nothing was against her will. I got so confused that I didn't know what to do.

———————

After the sounds had subsided, I left the apartment, not saying a word to anybody and decided that it would be better to brave the cold than stay there that night. Having another hour before being able to return home by bus, I decided to make my way to the train station. In general, train stations are the places in European cities where you can find all sorts of people during the night. There were homeless beggars, drug dealers, punks, and all kinds of riff-raff. I just remember how much attention I was attracting, looking young and innocent in comparison to the numerous homeless and punks. The train station in Innsbruck at four in the morning is not the place for a nineteen-year-old American.

There was a group of "*Gruftis*", at that time a type of gang in Austria, with their faces painted white, wearing black clothing. They were waving and smiling, trying to scare me and being quite successful at it. In addition to this, there was another group of people in the corner on the floor drinking beer and further a group of beggars sleeping on benches. *"What am I doing here?"* I thought anxiously.

Even though I was quite frightened and cold, an unusual thought came to mind. These exact kinds of experiences were probably the reason why I have always liked living abroad. In fact, I would have never found myself in a similar situation at home. I knew every single street in our little town and where you shouldn't go alone at night. Every single dangerous situation could be recognized and therefore avoided. Not so in Europe. It had not even crossed my mind that the train station would be an inappropriate place to wait in the middle of the night. Living abroad was challenging every day, even stressful. But there was always something new to be explored and experienced. This is probably due to the ignorance that only a foreigner in a far off land would have, yet it is this very nativity that protects people, making the simplest occurrences, dangerous or not, seem so exciting in the new atmosphere and new way of life.

At that moment, the police came around and, of all these strange looking people, they came directly towards me, demanding to see my passport. Not having any identification on me, I can still remember how nervous I was. Trying to explain to them, in German, that I lived there was quite a task. They wanted to see some identification and started making gestures for me to come with them. In a rush to pull everything out of my pockets, I showed them my homework that was given to me by my composition teacher at university. It was a copy of an exercise sheet that said 'Mozarteum' with a whole bunch of notes written on it. Luckily, they changed their minds and decided to let me be. It was not until later that I found out that they would have had the perfect right to take me to the police station and hold me there until I had been able to come up with some identification. What a night!

The next day, the first girl I had ever fallen in love with and I didn't talk about what had happened and pretended as if we hadn't gone out together that night. We remained friends, but that was all. Sometimes, even though I don't have any contact with her now, I find myself asking what became of her and if she had ever realized the feelings I had for her.

STUDENT LIFE

After a year in Innsbruck, moving to Salzburg to study at the main university was very exciting. The city is absolutely gorgeous. I think it is the most beautiful city in the whole world. A vast part of the city center is built in Baroque style, huge cathedrals, all ornamented and colorful next to medieval city houses with little windows, cuddled next to each other. Towering above the entire city, on a mountain, is *Hohensalzburg*, a gigantic castle looking over the area, making it look like a magical fairy tale land.

At that time, I found accommodations at what you call in German a *studentenheim*, which is like a dormitory for students, but located in the city and not at a university. In Europe, universities are not generally located on a campus like they are in the US, but are usually broken up into different buildings within the city. The *studentenheim* was like something out of a horror movie on account of the fact that everything was so old and dusty. The walls were green with yellow flowers painted on them. The wooden staircase seemed like it was going to fall in. The place was really in need of renovation, but it only cost one hundred sixty dollars a month for a double room, so it had to do.

Although I really liked the city, the only downfall had to do with the people from there. Yes, I had already made friends with so many people from other places, but never really met anyone originally from Salzburg. I was told later by some acquaintances that the Salzburgers tend to keep to themselves. It was considered to be a very closed culture. The beauty of the city made up for it though.

Even though many of the Salzburgers weren't very friendly, I found out that it was not very difficult to get to know people coming from the city's vast international community as well as Austrians from various other cities. After living there for several years, I even met some of my best friends.

My student life in Salzburg was full of going out, drinking, talking about politics, meeting new people, and studying together in parks and coffee houses. It struck me as being very strange that students would even meet for a beer before classes, not thinking anything of it.

Drinking in Austria was a culture of its own. If I'd been a non-drinker, it would have been quite difficult. If someone had a birthday party, passed a test at university, or cooked something really special, there was always a reason to crack open a bottle of wine or grab a beer. In addition to drinking, there are a few rules that you have to follow or Austrians get angry. Here are the rules one has to absolutely abide by:

1. After the beer or wine is poured, you are not allowed to drink a single drop without saying "*prost*" and making a toast to each and every friend you are with.

2. While saying "*prost*", it is imperative that you look into each other's eyes. If not, this results in directly insulting your friends.

3. This process is obligatory every time a person is served a new drink and is sometimes repeated numerous times during a single drink for no reason whatsoever.

All of this was new to me, and I did not realize how important it was at first, until the people I went out with started making fun of me because I didn't obey those strange rules. I got used to them calling me an "*Ami*" that did not know how to drink beer. With time, I learned. To this very day, whenever I have a drink in *Ami-Land*, Austrian slang for the United States of America, friends and family look at me strangely, because now, I cannot stop saying cheers and looking into their eyes.

Drinking was something that could be done until the wee hours of the morning. Most of the pubs closed at four o'clock, but it was always possible to find a pub that stayed open much longer. There were even these mysterious black-market pubs that students flocked to because beer was sold for only a dollar a pint. In order to get into these pubs, it was normally necessary to ring a doorbell. Thinking about the possibility of the police raiding the place was also pretty exhilarating.

To go to a pub, it was always necessary to dress really well. The bouncers would only let you in if you had proper apparel on and only if they 'liked' you. There is a law in Austria that says that the owner of the pub can always choose whom he wants to come in and whom he can ban. This actually goes to the extreme of bouncers not letting you in account of the color of your skin, your nationality, or how you are dressed. That always bothered me quite a bit and I hope they will change this law some day.

Although supermarkets and shops closed between six and seven in the evening, it was never a problem to have a quick snack at night going from bar to bar with my friends. From dusk until dawn, there were numerous stands to buy all sorts of different types of sausages which are eaten with mustard, horse radish and a '*Semmel*', which is the Austrian word for a Kaiser Roll. There is something else called "*Leberkäse*," which for me, is nothing more than a hot dog in hamburger-form. It is normally served in a Kaiser Roll with a green pepper inside of it. I hated it, but to my astonishment, my Austrian friends couldn't eat enough of them.

Going out with several different people during this time made me realize how different Austrian conversation could be in comparison to chatting in

America. A discussion among Austrians was, in a word which describes it perfectly, pedantic. A group would start on a topic, like the president of the US, for example, and stay on the topic for a whole hour without talking about anything else. My friends would even go so far as to grab an encyclopedia and look something up if they weren't sure about it. I found this to be a trait that most Austrians have. After a while, it started rubbing off on me and I started doing it too. It made it easier to hang out with Austrian friends, but it has always driven my family in the US absolutely crazy because I never want to let a topic drop.

WIENER SCHNITZEL AND KEBAB

Whenever it was possible and if money wasn't too short, I would explore Austrian cuisine. Going to restaurants with friends was an interesting experience because of the various foods that Austrians craved. Liver dumplings, goulash, Wiener Schnitzel, to name a few.

There were a few Austrian dishes that I considered deserts because they contained sugar, but they were actually main courses. An example of this would be *Marillenknödel*. Potato dumplings with apricot jam and sugar sprinkled all over it. In Austria, this is a typical dinner and I couldn't understand why until someone explained to me that being a Catholic country, many families still follow the tradition of not eating meat on Fridays. It is for this reason that sweet dishes served as a main course have developed in traditional Austrian cuisine. These meals are vegetarian but still provide people with the energy they need. I really had to be careful what I ordered, because some of the food, in my opinion, was just horrible. I would order entire meals only to find out that I couldn't eat them. There was one food in particular, *Kasnockerl*, which I just could not stand. The dish consisted of thick flour noodles and several different types of cheeses in great masses. It is served hot and gooey. Not only could I not eat it, I could not even smell it.

Speaking of all this food makes me think about the person I had to share a room with. He was Austrian and liked cooking things on his hotplate, which had the consequence of our room always smelling like onions.

He was also a bodybuilder that loved speaking English. He went so far as to explain to me that he was not at all interested in what I had to say, but just wanted the practice. That has happened to me quite a few times. Many people have wanted to be my friends with the sole purpose of practicing their English. Courses for English conversation in Europe are very expensive. It is much cheaper to just find someone who speaks English and try to practice the language for free.

Having to speak English with him wasn't really the problem. This roommate was always walking around in his bikini underwear, even during the day. That bothered me quite a bit. On occasion, I invited friends from university up to the room for a chat and there he was, walking around half-naked. I found it extremely embarrassing. Although I had always asked him politely to get dressed, he never cared and did not seem to have an ounce of shame. Actually, even if he had been completely naked in the presence of my friends, I don't believe it would have concerned him at all.

Above all, there was one thing he did that drove me crazy. He would always leave the door to our room unlocked. I had all of my valuables including my guitar in our room. This didn't matter to him in the slightest, claiming that, "People don't steal in Austria."

It is true that the honesty I had been confronted with in Austria is a very nice aspect of living in the country. People are very true and it is generally quite safe. You could very easily leave your wallet full of money in the middle of the street and check at the police station later, only to find that someone turned it in without stealing a single cent. Unfortunately, this honesty leads most people to be quite good-hearted and, in my opinion, naive.

There are many Austrians, even today, that leave their doors unlocked at night or put their wallet on the table at a bar and leaving it while they go to the restroom.

A fellow student of mine got her purse stolen once. She came crying to everyone, "Someone took my purse." I thought she had just been mugged, listening to her babbling with panic, "I left my purse on the table of the restaurant and went to use the restroom and was only gone for five minutes. When I got back, my purse was gone!"

I had absolutely no sympathy for her at all. What she had just done, in my opinion, was absolute stupidity.

Getting used to living with my roommate was not impossible. I got used to the smell of onions in

our room when he cooked. Seeing him in his
underwear became completely natural, even for
my guests. After I locked him out a few times, he
started taking his key with him and locking the
door himself.

Despite all these great improvements, there
was one incident that was absolutely intolerable.
My roommate had a girlfriend and wanted her to
spend the night in the room with me in it! He
explained, "I just want her to be able to spend the
night, we won't make love, I promise."

"No," I exclaimed. "Do you think I am an
idiot?"

Well, we ended up making a compromise; he
could 'have' the room during the day when I was
out, as long as he put a sign on the door. He was
quite happy with my proposal, but there were
some pretty embarrassing moments every time he
forgot to hang up the sign. Yes, I absolutely hated
having a roommate and I despised what I had to
witness sometimes when opening the door,
unaware that he had "company". Nonetheless,
this is also something I got used to with time.

On each floor of our building, there were
about fifteen students and on the first floor there
was a huge kitchen where everybody cooked
together. It was a really old kitchen with an
adjoining dining room with some picnic tables and
benches to sit at. There was nothing else in the
kitchen except a counter to prepare the food, a
sink, a couple electric burners, and a couple of
huge refrigerators. Each person had a pad lock for
his own compartment in the fridge. That way it

wouldn't be possible to steal food from the many students living there. Oh, but did I mention, "People don't steal in Austria."

———————

One day, while cooking in the kitchen, I met a young man, about my age, making chicken for dinner. Arabic music was playing really loud on a small cassette recorder on the counter. I greeted him in German but he did not understand me.

"Where are you from?" he asked.

"The US, and you?" I answered.

"I am from Cairo. My name is Waeil."

It was the first time I had ever met anyone from Egypt. My mother and father had been to Egypt. It was the one huge trip that they went on and they filled my mind with views of the pyramids, camels, and all the beauty that the country had to offer. Standing right in front of me was a true Egyptian and I was just in awe. There were so many things I wanted to ask him about where he came from to see if my mother had really been telling me the truth all of these years about his country, when he beat me to the punch and asked, "Do you want a cigarette?"

I said, "Sure!" and took one from his package. Although I wasn't quite expecting that to be the first thing he'd ask, I lit it and said, "Thank you."

He retorted almost angered, "Why? It is just a cigarette!"

I didn't quite understand what he had meant by that, but then he told me that an Arab would never thank someone for a cigarette because it went without saying that I could have one. This struck me as being a bit odd, but then again, I had also never been introduced to the hospitality of an Arab. I told him that not saying "thank you" in the US would be considered pretty rude, which seemed just as strange to him.

Suddenly, a friend of his came in and started speaking the strangest language I think I had ever heard in my life. It sounded guttural, as if someone was trying to talk while being choked at the neck, but at the same time, there was a beauty to it. I asked this person if he was from Egypt too and if the language they were speaking was Egyptian. Well, as it turned out, Waeil's friend was from Libya and that day was the first time I had ever heard the Arabic language.

Over the next few days, I kept meeting Waeil in the kitchen or knocking on his door to visit him and have a cigarette. Since I had come to Austria, I had actually quit smoking, but in reality I had just quit buying my own.

This time, Waeil was sketching on a piece of paper and I asked him what he was drawing. "I am not drawing. I am writing a letter to my family," he said.

I looked at the paper and noticed that all it looked like was a bunch of scribbling and found it quite difficult to believe that his family could actually read it. In addition, it occurred to me that he was writing from right to left, which baffled me even more.

"Could you show me how to write in

Arabic?" I asked being the curious person I always was, "I'd like to learn it."

"You can't just learn it, it takes years. But if you want, I can try to show you," Waeil said. He started writing down the alphabet on a separate piece of paper. I have to say that Arabic writing fascinated me even more than the spoken language. Each letter was like a little drawing that was written in a type of cursive with all of the letters connected. Needless to say, it wouldn't have been possible to learn it in one day, but having been explained the structure, it was the incentive to later buy a book and start learning.

During our writing lesson, I had asked Waeil, "Can I have another cigarette?" It was at this moment that he finally asked me why I didn't ever go out and get my own. I felt a bit guilty and took some money from my pocket, saying that I was sorry, and gave him enough to buy another package.

He stared at the money I put on the table for a moment a bit dumbfound, took the bills into his hand and ripped them. He was furious! "Why do you give me money!" he said, getting up and literally throwing me out of his room. Standing there shaking in front of his closed door, I had no idea what I had done wrong. I thought that I was just paying him back.

Later, in the kitchen, I demanded an explanation. He told me that no one had ever done something so rude to him in his life. After talking about it for a while, we came to the conclusion that it was a big misunderstanding. In his culture, what I had just done was insulting on account of the fact that you don't ever offer an Arab money in exchange for his hospitality. I told him that in the US, it wouldn't matter in the slightest if a friend gave me a few bucks for a package of cigarettes. "In my opinion, your reaction was truly uncalled for," I said. After apologizing to each other, we realized that we were both foreigners in a foreign land and had a lot to learn about cultures.

As time went by, I started learning Waeil's language from a book and got to know quite a few people from several Arabic countries through my new best friend. I met people from Morocco, Algeria, Tunisia, and all over North Africa and the Middle East. It was actually one of the most interesting times I had ever had in Austria, getting to know so many people from so many different far off countries. Even though I was learning the language on my own, I could always go to them if I had a question and they were happy to help me.

When we went out we used to eat kebab, a form of fast food that you can get just about everywhere in Austria, and is especially loved by people with Middle Eastern backgrounds. It is exactly like a Greek gyros, except with lamb or chicken instead of pork.

Having been invited to dinner on a number of occasions by my new friends, Arabic food and the Islamic religion were gradually introduced to me for the first time. I learned to eat things with my right hand as well as how to cook things that I would have never imagined. Although I was not Muslim, my friends taught me the basic principles of Islam and how to pray. A whole new world of culture had been opened up to me. I, in turn, showed them how to make chili, chocolate chip cookies and brownies, gradually introducing them to the basics of US living. It was a great trade off.

Unfortunately, amongst my Arab friends, I had been confronted with all of the prejudices they had to face in Austria. I had been a person living in Austria by choice. With the exception of Waeil, who was a student, these people, most of them refugees, had been forced to leave their countries to seek asylum from the Austrian nation. This changed my whole outlook on life. Up until that point, I thought I understood Austria and its people quite well. Through these friends, I saw a side of Austria that I would have never expected. I was witness to unbelievable examples of racism. Many of my friends had difficulties finding a room to stay; they were ignored on the streets and if they weren't, they were ridiculed.

Sometimes, going into shops, I noticed that they had difficulties getting waited on. Of course, there were even people who did not like me because I was an American, but before I opened my mouth and my accent was heard, I could have very easily been taken for one of them. My friends, however, had dark skin and were seen right away as being Arab. Accompanying them through the city, most people presumed that I had also been an Arab and treated me in the same way.

It was horrible. By the way, this was years before September 11.

There is a lot of racism in the US, but, in Europe, it is not skin color alone, it has to do with religion and wealth also. The people from Eastern Europe are also looked down on because the economic situation in their respective countries is poor. A lot of them come for work and a better life. Many Arabs come for those reasons, yet a great few come on account of political reasons and not economic ones. It must be really difficult for them to have to leave their families in order to find safety and security in their daily lives.

During this time, the information I learned about political refugees just horrified me. They were not allowed to work until they were accepted for asylum, so it was very difficult for them to survive. Some of them were supported by their families at home and some didn't have anything at all. They are all dependent on each other and, at the same time, each is completely alone. Their strength is to stick together as a group and be survivors.

Listening how some of them traveled to Austria and the hardships they had to endure was unbelievable. I had thought that I, up until that point, had seen and done so much, but listening to their experiences really made me feel like a child that had not yet seen anything of the world.

Much later in life I found out, to my surprise, that many political refugees exist in the US as well, and have the exact same problems. Living abroad you get to see and experience things that you wouldn't even be aware of in your own country, until seeing them from a distance.

I learned from all my new friends how important it was to understand different cultures and have a deeper understanding for people in tough situations. That is the only way to help humanity, no matter where a person is from. After learning a great deal about the Arabic culture, I was not only accepted by them as an equal, but as a brother.

It is a fact that a person needs family. Living abroad on my own, I had been taken in by many people. Many of my friends became brothers and sisters. There were also older people that I considered my mothers and fathers. I don't think I have ever had such close friendships as I have had in those first few years alone.

Looking back at the topic of food, which originally brought me to think about the kitchen in the first place, presently, after having lived in the country for many years now, there is very little Austrian food that I don't like. In fact my personal favorites are *Kasnockerl* and *Leberkäse*. I must have acquired the taste for all of these delicacies. Eating foreign food is similar to making friendships abroad. It's just a matter of getting used to, trying new things, and being open.

VISITING MY FRIEND WAEIL FROM UNIVERSITY

Getting off the plane at about one o'clock in the morning, I still remember how orange everything looked. It was dark, but the sky was orange. Once again, I noticed that even this country had a foreign odor lingering in the air. It was the smell of spices and dust, food cooking and perfume. It wasn't overwhelming, but it was definitely present.

When my flight started in Munich, Germany, it was snowing outside. Arriving in North Africa, the fresh warm and arid air brushed into my face as soon as I exited the plane. I heard an Arabic woman speaking over the loudspeaker. This was the first time that I had ever heard a woman speaking the language. At that moment, it occurred to me that I had never had the chance to meet an Arabic woman and was not familiar with what a female Arabic voice sounded like. Very seldom does an Arabic woman travel alone, much less travel abroad.

I had been looking forward to my trip to Cairo

for what seemed like an eternity. Waeil invited me to meet him and stay with his family for a few weeks. Having been learning Arabic for about a year now, I was really excited about being able to use it. Right when I went up to get the stamp in my passport at the border control, I told the immigration officer that I already had a tourist visa for Egypt in my passport in his native tongue, *"Andi taschiirati fil-jawaazis-safarii."*

My eyes met up with his again and he said in a voice just like Waeil's, "You speak Arabic? Why? One moment!" With a waving gesture, two officials came and asked me to open my suitcase. Rampaging through my personal things, they took everything out and put everything back in again. I was horrified.

"Are you traveling alone?" they asked. "Why are you traveling alone?"

They obviously became very suspicious because of my Arabic skills, which had improved quite a bit since my first Arabic lesson with Waeil. I guess it was quite odd that a twenty-one-year old American traveling alone would get off the plane and speak the language. On top of that, in my American passport, I had quite a few Austrian student visas and a tourist visa issued by the Embassy of Egypt in Vienna, which I had applied for in order to not have any complications upon entry into the country. It actually made matters worse. Anything out of the ordinary is considered a possible security threat.

"Where do you stay? Who you meet here?" the immigration officers asked.

"I am meeting my friend who is from here. He is supposed to pick me up at the airport," I said.

"What is his name, where does he live?" they asked briskly.

Then, my heart almost quit beating as it occurred to me that I did not even know where my friend lived, nor did I know his last name. For me, he was just my buddy Waeil. After a series of questions and me almost starting to cry, they ended up letting me go on through the customs gate after having looked through my suitcase a second time.

After going through customs, as you can probably imagine, I was a bit shaken up, only to find that there were thousands of people in the airport, all dressed in beige robes. I felt like I had just stepped out of a space ship. Everything looked so ancient and mysterious, from the way people were dressed to the writing on the old walls of the airport. There were people screaming so loudly, it was as if they were screaming right into my face, "Taxi, you need TAXI?!" Suddenly, someone grabbed me and started pulling me in the direction of the exit doors wanting to drag me outside to their taxi. I was absolutely full of fear. Waeil was nowhere to be seen.

I kept telling them in Arabic that my friend was coming to pick me up. They asked me, "Who is your friend. What is his name?" At this moment, I was praying that Waeil would soon appear. I do not know what I would have done if he hadn't.

After waiting for about five minutes, which seemed like an hour because I was being driven crazy by everyone, a man came up and helped me, commanding all of the men to leave me alone. He was an official who seemed to be very nice. Then he turned to me smiling and asked, "Who are you waiting for? What is his name? Give me his telephone number. Open your luggage!" At this moment, I saw Waeil and started screaming his name. He came and rescued me from what seemed to be the most fearful moment of my whole life. He explained to the official that I was his guest and that there was nothing to worry about.

"Do you need cigarettes?" Waeil asked. "Come!" He then led me to a cave-looking place in the middle of the airport that looked like something out the middle ages. It was just a stone hole in the wall where a feeble little man in rags was selling his wares. I wanted to buy some cigarettes from him but realized that I didn't have any Egyptian currency yet.

"Michael, it is better if you let me buy things for you here. Tourists are thought to have a lot of money, so people will raise the prices to cheat you," Waeil said, "They will not do this to me because I am Egyptian." Waeil took some notes out of his pocket and paid. Thinking about what once happened when I tried to pay Waeil back for cigarettes in Salzburg, I was not sure when I'd be able to pay him back.

We exited the airport. As I finally took in a breath of fresh air, I was shocked to see how many cars there were on the street and how loud everything was. There were horns honking and people yelling out of the windows of their vehicles. As we were walking toward the sidewalk, Waeil gave a loud whistle that almost hurt my ears and a taxi pulled over from the ongoing traffic at the sidewalk before we even got there.

Getting into this black taxi, that looked like it was going to fall apart, gazing at the masses of people, I started glancing around and noticed the orange light of the street lamps, the black and white markings on the sidewalk and the donkey carts driving alongside the cars on the street. After we were on the road, I left everything up to Waeil to get us to his home. I was completely intimidated and overwhelmed by everything to the extent of feeling ill. We drove for about five minutes and the taxi driver pulled something out of his pocket which turned out to be a package of cigarettes and offered one to each of us. After lighting up, I was a bit unsure about where to ash the cigarette, as all the windows were closed and I could not open them. Waeil told me, "You are in Cairo now," as he ashed on the floor of the taxi.

———————

Although it didn't feel at all comfortable, I sat there smoking the cigarette and ashing onto the floor of the vehicle, looking out the window, listening to the driver and Waeil speaking Arabic at full speed and getting lost in my own thoughts. I was just amazed. All the buildings were made of stone with flat roofs. In the distance, I could identify the mosques with their minarets rising high up into the sky. It was the strangest, most beautiful thing I had ever seen. As the car drove on, we passed people wearing rags, stands on the street selling food, and people traveling by donkey carrying large loads of food and what seemed to be junk. The streets were filled with a bunch of beat up old cars, but mixed amongst this chaos were also the most expensive cars and limousines I had ever laid my eyes upon. Above all, there were so many black taxis everywhere with Arabic written all over them. The various drivers were screaming out of the windows to make the traffic move along faster. Although the atmosphere actually scared me, it was a rush of excitement that will never be forgotten.

At a moment's notice, Waeil started violently yelling at the taxi driver, making him stop on the side of the road. I didn't know what was happening. I was told to get my things from the back of the taxi right away, "We go now," Waeil said. We were in the middle of a highway! As the taxi driver drove away yelling things at us in a way that made me fear the language, I heard a loud whistle that almost hurt my eardrums and another taxi stopped at the side of the road to pick us up.

After we got in, Waeil explained that the other taxi driver did not **agree** to his price. I mentioned the fact that there **was** a meter in the taxi and wondered why it had presented a problem. "That's only for **tourists** and it is meant to cheat them," he said. "In Cairo," he explained, "you have to know how far you are traveling and bargain for a good price."

To my surprise, thinking that the previous driver had been an exceptionally generous person, the second taxi driver pulled a package out of his shirt and asked us, "Do you want to smoke?" wanting to try out his English, handing us both a cigarette smiling.

"People here really smoke a lot," I thought. Waeil then explained that most taxi drivers offer a cigarette to their passengers out of respect.

After a really long drive, the taxi finally stopped in front of a big old stone building where we were greeted by about three people on the street, all looking at me curiously and greeting me with, "Welcome to Cairo!"

It was about two o'clock in the morning. The people stared me up and down as if they were examining every inch of me, but couldn't say anything else in English except, "Welcome to Cairo," which must have been repeated at least twenty times. After saying goodbye to them, we entered the building and I asked Waeil who they were. He exclaimed, "They are friends that are curious about you coming to visit. It is not every day that an American comes to our neighborhood."

As we were walking up the stairs of what seemed to be an apartment building, I kept hearing screams of people yelling. It was really loud. And the strangest thing is that there were cats everywhere. I had never seen so many cats in my life!

As the door to Waeil's home opened, an older

lady dressed in black with dark skin and beautiful brownish hair, obviously my friend's mother, stood in front of me. She glanced into my eyes and smiled. After looking down toward the suitcase I had in my hand, she started yelling at the top of her lungs at Waeil. She was inflamed that he let me carry my own suitcase. Waeil's little brother came to greet me saying, "Welcome to Cairo," and shaking my hand. His mother started yelling at him, causing him to immediately take my suitcase and disappear with it. I was a bit confused and, above all, terribly tired!

Waeil asked me if I was hungry and told me that his mother was making food for us. I said, "It is two o'clock in the morning. I don't need anything to eat."

"You must eat something, Michael, my mother is cooking," he said.

"No, really, that is okay. I am really not hungry at all," I said.

Looking at me very concerned he said, "I don't know how to explain this to you Michael. You must eat something. It is our way. When someone new comes into the house, you are our guest and you must eat. If you don't eat something, my mother will be very insulted and I have no doubt that she will want to throw you out of our house on to the street. So, please eat something." This statement made me think of the first experience I had had with Waeil in Salzburg when he threw me out of his room because I gave him money.

We sat down at the table and I heard his

mother cooking away. After a few minutes, she came in with a platter of beans and a platter of French fries. A few seconds later, she arrived with a plate full of hamburgers. Seeing that I was an American guest, she wanted to cook something she was positive I would like. Hearing the sound of grease in the kitchen once more, my face turned completely white. I looked at my friend who was smiling at me with content. I whispered asking him, "How am I going to eat all this? Is she still cooking?"

"It is our way," he said, "Eat as much as you can and don't worry about eating everything. If you were able to eat it all, my mother would feel like she was insulting you. That would probably result in her wanting to throw you out."

While eating, I looked around the apartment. The walls were a bit run down, but the furniture, especially in the living room, was very beautiful. There were chairs that were brushed in gold and the table looked like it had been hand carved. On the table were brass figures that made everything look as if we were in a museum. The floors of the apartment were made of stone, but there were beautiful rugs everywhere.

After the meal, which was out of this world, it must have been around three or four o'clock in the morning and Waeil asked me if I wanted to go for a coffee and play pool with his friends. Although I was tired and wasn't really expecting to go anywhere that evening, I was quite pleased because I was really curious about what was outside. I went looking for my suitcase only to see

Waeil's little brother standing next to it opened with my clothes all over the bed. I was a little bewildered and didn't know what to think until I realized what he was doing.

He was ironing my clothes and putting them into a closet. I was completely stunned and said that it wasn't necessary, trying to get him to stop ironing. He did not understand me and continued because these were his mother's orders. I have never been encountered with such hospitality again throughout my whole life.

Drinking coffee and playing pool during the early hours of the morning was really exciting. In Egypt, it is common to drink Turkish coffee, which is coffee that is made by melting the grounds into the water and adding sugar. I found its taste much different to filter coffee, but it was quite delicious. Above all, I really needed something to be able to stay up so late and wow, was that coffee strong! We also ordered a water pipe with tobacco that smelled like apples. There were so many new tastes and smells that I was confronted with that it was almost difficult to process them in my mind.

We went to bed at the crack of dawn. It was then, that I realized that there was only one king-size bed for all of the men in the house. Waeil had three brothers. The eldest slept on the floor so I could sleep in the bed. Before being invited, no one told me that I would have to sleep in a bed with three other people. In the beginning, I was horrified, but I got used to it with time. It was only later that I realized how kind it was of Waeil to have invited me. An invitation in Egypt is taken very seriously and is not something that is given lightly.

———————

The next morning, I was woken up by the calling of the mosques, which was absolutely ethereal. I got up and went looking for Waeil. He was standing on the balcony outside in the sun drinking tea with milk. It was about noon. He asked if I wanted a cup and my heart almost skipped a beat when I realized what was in the distance. From his balcony, you could see the tip of the Great Pyramid of Giza. "Incredible," I said with my mouth dropped and my eyes ripped wide open.

Entering the bathroom, I noticed that it was completely made of stone covered with tiles. There was a drain in the middle of the floor and it was wet everywhere. For this reason, Waeil had me put on slippers before entering. There was no toilet paper but a hose attached to the toilet that spurted water with such pressure that I actually had to change my jeans after cleaning my backside. It was so embarrassing. Seeing that I could never get used to this hose, the family ended up buying toilet paper just for me. Before I took a shower, Waeil's brother had to come and light a pilot light to heat the water. As I stood there washing myself, I will never forget looking at the open flame and watching the water trickle down into the drain in the middle of the bathroom.

That day, we met several of Waeil's friends and they took me to visit the pyramids. It was very sunny and hot outside. One of his friends came to pick us all up by car. There were about six people stuffed into one vehicle, Egyptian music was blaring and they all pulled out little tiny cymbals and rhythm instruments and started playing along with the music. It was astounding. As we were driving along, one of the friends said, "Michael, look! The pyramids!" Strangely enough, the pyramids were not as exciting as I expected in comparison to the cultural experience that I was having and had had up to that point. The great afternoon I was having with all of Waeil's friends made the pyramids seem insignificant.

On the way home, we had to buy some chicken for dinner. We walked into what looked like a pet shop with a lot of animals in cages. After walking in, I found out that we actually just entered a butcher's, who took a live chicken and slaughtered it before my eyes. My hands were shaking as I carried the bag of chicken back to Waeil's house. I think that was the freshest chicken I have ever eaten, although the way we had purchased it was a bit frightening.

It wasn't until one evening when a group of acquaintances were driving me around the city without Waeil that things started getting a bit scary. We all went for a drive and stopped in kind of a dark alley. A joint got taken out and passed around. I remember not feeling at ease, but I couldn't just get out of the car because I had no idea where I was. In Arabic countries, alcohol is forbidden legally and morally, but many smoke marijuana and do not think anything of it, even though it is also officially illegal. It was very dark out and suddenly there was a big spotlight on us.

I asked the friend squished next to me in the backseat what was going on. "*Hukuma*," he said. What he had just said scared the living daylights out of me. *Hukuma* in Arabic means 'government'. In that moment, I saw my whole life pass before me. I was going to spend a lifetime in an Egyptian prison. The sight of the prisoners in chains doing manual labor on the street a few days before crossed my mind.

A man started approaching us, who, all of a sudden, broke out laughing. He was a police officer, but he was also a friend of one of the people in our car. It was a joke. As the police officer grabbed the joint to take a drag off of it, I was speechless.

After about a week, I was getting tired of making hand gestures with people to communicate and was dying to speak English. Waeil called one of his friends who happened to be in town. It turned out she was from Australia but her mother lived in Cairo. It was very interesting to meet her because she was able to not only speak English with me but also translate everything I wanted to tell all of my new friends in perfect Arabic. It was a truly wonderful day. We ended up staying out until about eleven o'clock at night. While taking her home, she insisted on paying for the taxi. The taxi driver would not accept her money. He said that there were three men in his taxi and he would not accept money from a woman. We were forced to pay.

As I was saying goodbye to my new Australian friend, I kissed her on the cheeks. In Austria, you always say goodbye to good female friends with kisses on both cheeks and in Cairo, men greet and say goodbye kissing each other on the cheeks as well. I did it without even thinking. At a moment's notice, a huge spotlight was on us both and a man was yelling at us from on top of a tower using a loud horn. I couldn't understand a word he was saying.

"Michael! Talk English really loud!" she hissed giving me the impression that something was wrong. "Okay Michael, I'll see you in New York!" she started screaming at me with a very white look in her face. The whole thing took me by such a surprise, I did not know what to think. Was she crazy?

"Take care, it was good seeing you! We'll see each other in the US!" I said and left the scene. The white light dyed out.

I will never forget saying goodbye to that woman in Cairo, and I mean never. Only afterwards did I find out in what a dangerous situation I had brought myself into without knowing it. Waeil explained to me what was going on and seemed really nervous. The man shouting was actually a police officer who thought that I was an Arab boy from the neighborhood. Having seen me give kisses on the cheeks of a neighborhood girl, he was extremely shocked and started screaming over the loudspeaker that he was about to shoot me with his machine gun.

That was the most interesting trip I had ever made, but I left soon afterwards. Luckily, I didn't end up in jail and I wasn't shot. I really had a great time though.

SELF DIAGNOSIS AND GOING TO THE DOCTOR

In Salzburg, after eventually moving out of the student residence, I found a room located in the attic of a little wooden house with three other students. We each had a room with a desk, a bed, a sink, and a hotplate. We always called them mini-apartments. These rooms were incredibly small but they were really inexpensive and had everything a student would need.

If we needed anything other than what we had, all we had to do was ask our landlord, who was one of the kindest people I have ever known in Austria. He didn't just rent the rooms to make money, but really wanted to help students out by offering an inexpensive place to stay.

Every month, we had to pay the rent in person, which entailed going next door to where he and his wife lived. It was always a lot of fun because he was really curious about our lives. Paying the rent usually took a whole evening. Each and every time, I remember getting invited to eat and it became commonplace for my landlord and his wife, who were in their early eighties, to break open a bottle of wine or hard liquor and talk for hours about how Austria and my studies had been treating me.

They both became my family and truly looked out for me. I still refer to them this day as "*Oma*" and "*Opa*", the German words for grandma and grandpa. I don't think I could have ever afforded to go to school or actually enjoyed my stay in Europe for so long if I hadn't found that room.

The other students I lived with became my good friends and we formed our own type of family. We always told each other where we were going and tried to keep ourselves out of trouble. There was Waeil who had moved into the same house, my friend Erika from Slovakia, and Sebastian from France. We were all young and carefree and knew how to live. There were a lot of parties, friends, and eating. It was like paradise. There was only one catch to the whole thing. There was a tiny bathroom and a tiny shower that we had to share everyday.

Sharing a bathroom is not the end of the world. We tried to keep it clean whenever we could, but with so many people using it, it was probably not the most hygienic place in the world. I started getting an itch in my groin that would not go away. I never went to the doctor for it, because I thought I had a simple case of jock itch.

It was not until one evening when I started examining myself under an arm-lamp. I wanted to see if it was just a rash or something else that was causing this itching that was getting worse as time went by. Looking closer, I saw something move and then everything went black. I had passed out. When I came to my senses, I realized what was causing the itch and did not want to look at it again.

I knew exactly why I had reacted the way I did. As a young boy, my mother had a hair and wig salon. She had always checked us for lice on a weekly basis, saying that it would be bad for business if we ever got it. On account of these memories during my youth, in my mind, I had not just contracted body lice, it was as if I had just been stricken with some sort of disease.

It was two o'clock in the morning and I was afraid to fall asleep and waited until eight o'clock for the pharmacies to open. For some strange reason, I kept thinking that they would eat me up if I went to sleep.

I was there when the pharmacy opened. Unfortunately, I was not the only customer and had to wait my turn. As the lady asked me what I needed, I asked, "Yes, do you have anything for lice?"

"Yes, of course we do," she said as I noticed the man and the lady who were behind me. They both took two steps away from me, fearing that they might catch something. The lady explained, "With this shampoo, you have to rub it into the scalp very thoroughly and leave it on...," suddenly stopping in the middle of her sentence when she saw my face getting so red. "What is the matter?" she asked.

"If possible, I'd like to speak to you alone," I

pleaded.

"What do you need?" she asked abruptly.

"The lice is not on... my head," I exclaimed, witnessing the faces of everyone surrounding me just drop, open-mouthed in horror. It was very embarrassing.

"One moment, I have to check to see if this works for THAT too. We also have a spray," she said.

"I'll take them both." After paying, I left the pharmacy never to return to that particular one ever again.

Coming back home and having to explain to everyone was the worst part of it. The pharmacist had made sure to tell me that I wasn't the only one affected, but everyone that was in contact with our toilet. That meant that everyone on the whole floor had to be treated. My roommates refused to believe that they could be afflicted by such a thing and denied having anything at all, telling me that they were not going to use the medicated shampoo. Who wants to admit that they have crotch crabs! Nevertheless, I left the shampoo in the bathroom and saw that it dwindled down with time as my roommates inconspicuously used it. My friends and I were cured soon after. After that, we always kept a bottle of disinfectant near the toilet and made sure to spray the seat before sitting down. "*At least, I didn't have to go to the doctor*," I thought.

I managed to avoid going to the doctor in Austria for a long time. It constantly bothered me that you could never get allergy pills or flu medication over the counter. Whenever I asked for it, the pharmacist said, "No, I am so sorry, I can give you aspirin, but for any stronger than that, you'll need a prescription." I didn't have a great deal of money and was always afraid of going to the doctor out of fear that it would be too expensive. It was for this reason that I stocked up on over the counter medication whenever I went back to the US or had my family send me some. This basically meant that every time I got sick, I tried to cure myself.

It was not until I started getting a growth on my neck that looked like a tumor that I had to break down and go to the doctor. It then occurred to me that I did not even know where to go or how to do it. I was paying some sort of obligatory insurance every month which amounted to about twenty dollars, but was afraid of going to the doctor and having that amount rise to the point that I couldn't afford it. Seeing this growth in my neck, I had no choice but to find out how going to the doctor in Europe functioned.

I went to my landlord, asking him for his advice and what I had to do to go to the doctor. He explained to me that I only had to go to the insurance agency and pick up a piece of paper which allowed me to go to the doctor of my choice.

At the insurance agency, which was a governmental building, it was very intimidating.

There were plain and green walls everywhere, as was every governmental building in Austria. For this reason, it was difficult to know where to go and I was always forced to ask someone.

After being told where and what line to stand in, it occurred to me how many people in line just looked ill. We were all doing exactly the same thing, namely waiting to pick up this sheet of paper to go to the doctor. What was I getting myself into? Having to wait about an hour before receiving my piece of paper and after showing my identity card and filling out a form, I wished I was back in the US.

They informed me that it was necessary to pay a three-euro processing fee and I started getting worried about all the money I would end up paying by the time all of this was over. It scared me to death to think that I might not be able to finish my studies because of getting myself into such a financial situation.

Leaving this institution and getting this piece of paper that looked a little bit like a shop invoice, I asked where the nearest doctor was and went there, having no idea who or how good he was.

My first visit to the doctor was really scary. Walking into his office was like walking into an apartment, even though it said that it was a doctor's office on the door. A man in the waiting room had an I.V. in his arm and another man was hooked up to some sort of machine. After signing up at a type of reception area, I waited for the doctor to come out and call my name. I was incredibly nervous, never having set foot in a doctor's office abroad before. I had heard a lot of horror stories and did not want to become a victim of malpractice, nor did I want to become a poor man doing so. There was a man sitting next to me in the waiting room that smelled atrocious, which didn't make matters any better.

The doctor called me in and asked me a lot of questions. Among his questions were how long it had been since I had gone to the doctor. I had to admit to him that I had not been to the doctor for many years. In the US, I didn't have any insurance and if I got sick, I just went to a walk-in clinic. He could not understand this at all and started printing out a lot of sheets of paper. He then gave me a handful of invoice looking papers and told me that they were to go see a lot of other doctors and laboratories. He wanted my blood tested, my eyes tested, x-rays, and a lot of other things that I didn't even understand at the time.

The sheets of paper were like coupons for each respective doctor. It was at this moment that I began to tell him that I could never afford to go to all these doctors. I was, after all, alone and did not have that much money. I also informed him that I could not afford it if they raised my insurance. I left the coupons on his desk and was about to leave when he said, "What do you mean? You are in Austria. It doesn't cost anything to go to the doctor."

I couldn't believe my ears! I instantly took the coupons and put them into my pocket and smiled. After thanking the doctor, I left on my way to make an array of appointments with more doctors than I had ever seen in the past ten years.

I ended up having an operation to take out a cyst in my neck. At first, I thought it was a tumor, but it turned out to be a harmless water-filled growth, which I really can't explain. Being in the hospital was an interesting experience. It was not like going to the hospital in the United States. It was clean, but extremely homey. Each room looked like a little apartment with several beds. There was no television, but a telephone and a wooden cross with a depiction of Jesus on it.

The nurses were very nice and lots of people came to visit me. At that time, I was teaching German to a Syrian I had met. He needed to learn the language to be able to get a job in Austria. Offering to teach him what I knew about the language for free, I wasn't expecting a thing from him. In fact, I enjoyed the company, which took away my boredom. He insisted on bringing me home-cooked food his wife had made.

The nurses did not like him very much because he wasn't able to communicate with them very well. He was an imam, an Islamic priest, who, facing east, prayed five times a day in the corner of my hospital room, which I shared with four other people. Somehow, the nurses felt very threatened by this and thought I was about the strangest patient that they had ever met. To sum things up, I was an American teaching German to a Syrian Islamic priest.

During this time, I also got to know several people from Iraq. Shortly before going to the hospital, I became acquainted with them through the Arabic club I joined, after having been introduced by my friend Waeil. I had explained to them how afraid I was about having my operation, so they came to visit me in the hospital quite often, which added to the nurses' worries.

Amongst themselves, the nurses kept asking why an American would have so many Arabic friends. I once tried to explain it to them. Both the Arabs and I had something in common. In Austria we were both foreigners and we were all alone. In general, our friendship happened by chance, but I am sure glad that it did because it opened up a whole new culture to me.

Without a doubt, the most memorable person of this group was my best friend Wisam, who not only taught me a lot of the Arabic language and culture, but also about his perspective on life. He is a person who enjoys life no matter the situation, and has always tried to find humor in everything. I will never forget his frequent visits while I was in the hospital. Maybe he did this because he didn't have anything else to do, but during this time, especially being without my family, it was very comforting to know that I was not alone. Later, he told me that it was because he heard me speaking on the phone with my mother shortly before the operation, telling her how afraid I was. During my two-week stay in the hospital, he ended up visiting me every day.

After finally being able to leave the hospital, Wisam and I continued to meet every day. We became the best of friends. The two of us often went out, chased women, and exchanged our thoughts. It was a lot of fun.

Although he was a great friend, I will never forget some of the crazy things he made me believe. One day, he made a strange remark, "Michael, why don't you have a beard? You have no hair on your face."

"No, I guess not," I said. "It used to bother me, but I don't care much about it now."

"I know a remedy for this that they use in Iraq, garlic. You must rub garlic into your face every day."

Hearing this, I thought my friend was joking with me. I had never heard of such a thing. He kept swearing to me that it would work. For some reason or another, I talked myself into going through with it, just to prove that it was nonsense. So every day, I let Wisam rub garlic onto my face with all of his might until my face was all blistered and I finally said, "Enough!"

I went to the doctor after that and he said that I was a moron for even trying such a thing. After confronting Wisam with what the doctor said, he told me that the doctor didn't know anything. Nevertheless, my garlic treatments came to an end.

———————

Not too long after my doctor experience, the dreadful day of September 11 occurred, shocking the world. I was in the United States with my family when it happened and my flight back to Austria was scheduled soon after. I was worried at the time that I wouldn't be able to fly back. I called my friend Waeil in Egypt and he told me that he had similar worries.

In Egypt, they had just issued a temporary law that said that men under the age of thirty-five were not allowed to travel by plane. Luckily, he got special permission from the Egyptian government on account of his studies to return to Austria. After worrying to death about it, I was also able to return to Austria.

After arriving back in Salzburg, I found myself watching television with a group of my friends from Iraq. They were watching a news station and the day of the military action "Shock and Awe" had arrived. This was the day that numerous bombs had been dropped on Baghdad. Coincidentally, all of my Iraqi friends came from that very city. As we watched the bombs fall on the news, we saw the buildings being destroyed with a continuous series of glowing lights from the sky while detonation after detonation took place. I was truly 'shocked and awed', as were many who watched this around the world.

I glanced away from the television and looked at my friends' faces glued to the screen. I not only saw horror in their faces, but also the fact that they were trying to keep from crying. I started imagining what it would be like to be in Austria watching my own city in the United States get bombed on television and thinking about the possibility that my family and friends could die in an instant. A few minutes later, my friends were all on their cell phones trying to reach their families with no avail. The lines were dead.

Living in the middle of these two worlds, Austria and Arabia, never made me feel more American. A person living abroad is faced with seeing how different the world is to his own. At the same time, the opinions I had been confronted with were not only pro- or anti- American, but the opinions of confused people expecting answers. Amongst all of my friends, I was known as *Michael the American*, and was forced to discuss, explain, and defend my way of thinking, my people, and the American way of life.

An American located in the US very rarely gets the chance or is in the situation of having to contemplate and justify the acts of his own country. The next day, not only my Arab friends, but also my Austrian friends interrogated me, to find out why the United States went to war. I felt as if I was representative of the United States and had to defend it. It is for this reason that I always keep up on politics; you never know when it will come in handy.

My parents told me afterwards that I should steer clear of my Arab friends. I told them that I had no intention of giving up my friends due to the actions of a few madmen. To my surprise, my Arab friends made it quite clear that they were not angry at me in the slightest. Arabs mainly come from totalitarian societies where the wishes of the government have nothing to do with what the people want. They were not mad at me, they were mad at my government. It still makes me contemplate if the phrase "We the People," still means something in the US.

A few days later, as I was walking away from my apartment with Wisam, who had come over for coffee, I started talking about the topic of my garlic treatments and how truly stupid he was. He said, "Michael, it will work, you will see." Then, at that moment, I saw someone in the distance, a very beautiful girl. She was walking away from the house next door. She had long blond hair and the most gorgeous features I had ever seen. My landlord had always talked about students living next door, but for the past two years, I had never had the opportunity to see or meet any of them. I was so stunned that I stopped talking with Wisam in the middle of my sentence. He, having noticed this, didn't hesitate a single moment and yelled at me saying, "What are you doing, you idiot, go and talk with her!"

She was on her way to the bus stop. Following Wisam's orders, I ran after her. As I ran behind her, at this time almost pursuing her, she started walking faster and faster, thinking I was some sort of freak. I finally met up with her in the bus and asked her name. It was love at first site. Without a doubt, she was the most beautiful girl I had ever seen and to my dismay, she didn't want to have anything to do with me, which made me think that I had to go to the doctor again on account of my broken heart.

———

Throughout my stay in Austria, I had gone to

the doctor many times for a lot of different things. I had to have my allergies taken care of and inserts made for my shoes because of my flat feet. A few months later, the doctor sent me to the dentist where I had two cavities filled and all four of my wisdom teeth taken out. To my surprise, at the time being completely oblivious to socialized medicine, nothing cost a thing except for processing fees of three euros every once in a while. My insurance always stayed at about twenty euros a month.

Lots of things happened during that time. My friend from Syria ended up speaking German very well and passed his test allowing him to work in Austria. He now works at a local mosque and people say that he still has an American accent when he speaks German but is very thankful to have had me as a teacher. My friend Wisam turned out to be the best friend I have ever had. About a month after my garlic treatments, I actually started growing a beard. The girl I met on the bus turned out to be an Austrian from Salzburg and became my girlfriend. Only about a year later, I asked for her hand in marriage.

LEARNING TO WALTZ FOR MY WIFE

The day before my wedding, we went to deliver the cake, which my mother made, to the reception hall located in the center of Salzburg. It was quite a chore because the cake was enormous and we had a very small car. My mother made that four-tier wedding cake all on her own. I was so proud of her, considering the fact that she brought about eight pounds of cake mix from the US just to make the cake for my wedding.

Everyone thought it was quite funny that she wanted to save room in her luggage by taking all of the cake mix bags out of their packages. Upon her arrival, she took several bags of white cake mix out of her luggage, explaining that she was going to bake for my wedding. It is a wonder that they did not suspect her of smuggling. It looked like her luggage was full of cocaine.

After dropping off the cake, my future mother-in-law took us back home and drove my fiancée, Katharina, to her sister's to spend the night. After all, it would be bad luck to see my wife before the wedding on the next day. I had a very wonderful evening with my mother. We talked, drank a bit of red wine on the patio and discussed our plans for the future. Expressing that I was looking forward to having children in Austria, my mother mentioned how worried she was about having to learn German in order to communicate with her grandkids. Thinking about two of my Austrian friends that were half American and raised bilingually, I told her not to worry.

We started talking about all the wedding preparations which we had made and how difficult everything was while still going to university and trying to juggle everything at once. My mother seemed pretty impressed.

My wife-to-be had hand-crafted all of the invitations with her friends. We sent out two hundred invitations and Katharina had cut out and painted every single one of them by hand. There was no doubt that she was set in her decision about getting married to me.

The next morning, the whole chapel and the reception hall were going to be decorated with flowers. Only two things were bothering me a little bit. I was worried about Katharina being kidnapped on the day of the wedding and the thought of having to waltz was killing me.

In Austria, there is a tradition that during the wedding reception, the bride is kidnapped by a group of friends and taken away to another pub for drinks. The groom is supposed to go out and find the bride. This can take hours and has been known to absolutely ruin weddings. Still, for Austrians, it is one of the most exciting parts of a reception. Thinking about everything really stressed me out. After all, I was told that I would not only have to find her, but also do some sort of game or test in order to win her back.

Besides that, I went into detail with my mother about how I had to learn to waltz. For an Austrian wedding, it is quite important for the bride and the groom to open up the dance floor by waltzing to the "Blue Danube" by Johann Strauss. This presents no difficulty to Austrians who generally all attend dancing school when they are sixteen years of age.

I had no idea how to waltz and asked my wife how she'd feel if I didn't dance for the wedding reception. She told me, "You have to learn."

From that moment on, I got books, videos, and people to show me how. I just couldn't manage to make never-ending circles and moving my feet in 3/4 time. It was absolutely hopeless. Most people get worried about the wedding itself; I on the other hand, was worried solely about the reception. It was not until a crazy evening with my best friend Luke when things started to finally crystallize.

My friend Luke, an Austrian-American, understood my dilemma perfectly. We sat on the porch of my apartment and had a couple of drinks together. My fiancée was inside drinking tea with a couple of friends. They were talking about the wedding and Katharina, I am sure, mentioned the difficulties I was having with learning to waltz.

She casually gazed out the window and saw me talking to Luke. A bit of time went by and she glanced in our direction once more and gasped with surprise. Luke and I were waltzing away on the porch. She and her friends came out and asked, "What are you guys doing?!"

Luke said, "I am teaching." We were both pretty drunk on the vodka we were drinking, but I have to admit, after that night, I finally learned to waltz.

———

On my wedding day, my mom and I got ready and then sat on the porch, had a bit of breakfast and drank a bit of coffee. I was really excited when we finally took a taxi into the city center.

There, I met up with my best man, who had coincidentally taught me to waltz, and we made our way to the registry office. In Austria, there are always two weddings, one in the registry hall for the State and one in the church for God. The registry hall in Salzburg is known to be one of the most beautiful in the whole world. It is all made of marble and brushed with gold, chandeliers on the high ceilings, and statues all around. It is, without a doubt, absolutely gorgeous. People come from many different countries around the world to get married there.

The car with Katharina drove in, with the horn honking wildly. I stood there waiting for her dressed in my black suit and tie as I helped her get out of the car, giving her a bouquet of flowers and a kiss. Looking at her gave me goose bumps because she truly looked like a princess in her sleek white wedding dress! We walked upstairs to the hall, passing by all of these beautiful marble statues of angels along the stairs. Waiting at the huge doors of the hall, getting ready to make our promise to spend the rest of our lives together, we were both absolutely filled with excitement.

Entering that room covered in marble with brushed gold and crystal chandeliers was exhilarating for us both. It was definitely a major turning point in my life. I could not believe that I was about to get married. After exchanging our vows and presenting each other with bands of gold, we went into the Mirabell Garden and had champagne in the open air. This is the garden where in the film *The Sound of Music,* the girl and the boy had kissed. For this reason, it is quite popular with tourists. It is also an important spot for the inhabitants of Salzburg. The Mirabell Garden with its Baroque statues and its collection of flowerbeds, is a meeting point and essential part of daily life and routine. On this spring day, it was the first day that all the Magnolias in Salzburg blossomed. Everything was as if it was just meant to be, absolutely perfect. Katharina's family started singing a traditional Austrian song. Having everyone around her singing in another language made my mother a bit nervous, but she went along with it and even started humming the song with them.

After getting married a second time in the church that afternoon, a white carriage led by white horses with an old man in a gray suit and top hat came to pick us up. We decided to take both of our mothers with us in the carriage so they could share the moment with us. Driving through the city, we attracted a lot of attention. We were waving to everyone we passed and many were yelling congratulations. A couple of Arab acquaintances I knew saw the carriage and ran into the middle of the street yelling in Arabic, "'*Mabruuk'* - Congratulations!"

Suddenly, I was having difficulty opening my eyes. It was an allergic reaction to the horses! My nose started itching and I started having trouble breathing. That is when I found out about my allergies. I thought my whole wedding was ruined. Luckily, it turned out that one of my wife's cousins, whom I had only met for the first time, was a doctor and just happened to have allergy medication. That was an incredible streak of luck. For this reason, I was still able to enjoy having cake and coffee, various games that were played, receiving gifts and having a nice dinner.

Suddenly, it happened. I heard the beginning bars of the "Blue Danube" waltz and I knew that this was our cue to go to the dance floor. The moment I had so anxiously anticipated had arrived. I met Katharina at the dance floor. The last time I had been able to waltz was with Luke on my porch, drunk on Vodka. This time I was completely sober, which made me quite nervous. We danced well and opened the dance floor with grace. The only thing I remember is starting to dance and finally leaving the dance floor.

A little while later, Katharina was gone. She had just disappeared. She had been kidnapped. I grabbed my friend Luke and a few other friends and we went into the city searching for her. I must have gone into five or six different pubs asking if they had seen my bride. It was not as bad as I thought it would be. A lot of people in the pubs laughed but were also aware that my bride had been kidnapped. Luckily, I did end up finding her because I had arranged for my best man, Luke, to be a spy. He knew what part of the city she was going to be in. If he had not done this, I would have looked for her for hours. I didn't really understand why the bride has to be kidnapped at an Austria wedding, but I went with the flow. After looking for her for an hour throughout the city, it was shocking when my wife, holding a glass of champagne in her hand, said "How did he find us so fast?" For her, this was the day of her wedding, and according to tradition, the one day in her life where she gets kidnapped and saved by her husband. She wanted it to last just a little longer. Looking at the excitement in her eyes, I finally understood more about Austria than I ever had before.

At the pub that she and her kidnappers were hiding out, they had a guitar ready for me. The kidnappers were not just going to give my wife back to me. In order to win Katharina back, I had to put strings on the guitar and play in the pub to earn enough money to cover all the champagne that had been drunk up to that point. Luckily, there just happened to be a huge group of women there celebrating a bachelorette party who got quite a kick out of the groom having to win back his bride. With two songs, to the surprise of everyone, I was able to earn about fifty euros.

I had never thought that my own wedding would turn out to be such a cultural challenge. It was great fun though. Getting into that plane to fly to Austria for the very first time as a seventeen-year-old, I was full of dreams. Never did I think that I would get married in Austria, yet it was like a dream come true.

THE SNAKE CHARMER

The day after our arrival in Spain, the idea of traveling to Morocco absolutely energized every bit of excitement in our bodies. Having spent the evening walking through the southern town of Algeciras, going out to eat, drinking wine, and watching the Statue of Maria being paraded through the streets, it seemed to be the perfect beginning to our honeymoon.

Getting on the Ferry was so exciting because it was my first time ever on such a big ship. It was equipped with a restaurant, a lounge, and even a casino. Setting up camp on the windy deck, it occurred to us that there were only about ten other guests on board. About half way to our destination, Arabic music started blaring throughout the whole ship. Our long awaited arrival was obviously getting nearer. We happened to meet a couple from England that was about our age. They were also planning on going to Marrakesh, a city located about ten hours by train from where we were about to arrive at. Looking out at the Strait of Gibraltar, we could finally recognize land off in the distance.

As the ship was docking, we saw several people all wearing robes. It was so dusty and there was foreign writing in every direction, written in Arabic and French. The first thing we had to do after getting off the ship was go to an ATM. As Katharina put her card through, a man behind her asked, "Do you need a taxi?" He was standing right next to her, looking over her shoulder! I impressed upon him that she did not need his help. Getting very angry with me, he started screaming right into my face. Not knowing how to react, after Katharina had withdrawn her money, we simply hurried away from the situation although it had really shaken us up. At once, memories of Egypt started coming to mind as the people continuously approached us, asking if we needed a taxi at the top of their lungs. This time my friend Waeil was not coming to pick me up as had been the case in Cairo. I was on my own this time and had a wife to care for.

As we were leaving the port on foot, I repeatedly told everyone that came up to us, "*Non, nous n'avons pas besoin d'un taxi – No we don't need a taxi*," although it didn't stop them from pestering us. The English couple, still not knowing how to react to this foreign atmosphere, was following us close behind. They were quite overwhelmed by the language barrier and had difficulty communicating. In Morocco, the first official language is Arabic, and the second official language is French. Although English can be used as a last resort, it is not commonly spoken.

After leaving the port and entering the city,

we headed right for the train station. We bought our tickets for the night train to Marrakesh and helped the English couple buy theirs as well, suggesting that we share a train compartment together. They were quite happy to agree.

We had thirteen hours before our train was scheduled to leave and therefore, a lot of time to explore Tangier. Seeing that our luggage was so heavy, we wanted to find out where we could lock it up so we could look around at ease. After finding out that the only place to store luggage was at the bus station located a few miles down the road, we decided to go there on foot and see a bit of the city in the process.

Looking around us, all the buildings were run down and there were many streets that weren't even paved. It started to really bother us that there were so many beggars on the street asking for money. They didn't just ask, but they followed us for quite a long way, pleading us to give them something. Some of them were also surprisingly young.

In our guide book, we were told that it wasn't good to give young people money because this would teach them that begging was a good thing and reinforce it. In lieu of this, the book suggested to give younger beggars pens so that they could use them in school. Despite our offerings of the various pens that we had ready and on hand, it did not seem to appease a single soul. In fact, it just made them angry.

Finally arriving at the bus station, the first thing that caught my attention was the fact that it was incredibly filthy. Unwashed people were begging on the floor, invalids with fresh wounds on their bodies looked into our eyes, holding out their hands asking for help, and to make matters worse, the whole area was covered by a film of thick dust. Right then, Katharina grabbed my arm and whispered to me quite discretely, "Michael, thank God we got all of our inoculations! Have you ever seen such a thing?"

After putting our luggage in safe keeping for a few hours, we went to our first Moroccan café. There was a cast-iron balcony looking over a market place. Looking at everything from above, we saw lots of people walking as well as numerous bicycles and motor scooters zooming around in every which direction. Even though the buildings looked like they were about to cave in, the sight of them was absolutely beautiful. The French had once colonized Morocco and the country is full of beautiful colonial-style architecture. Tangier had once been home to the well-off. In spite of its rough appearance, the city somehow had a lot of charm. Looking at the structure of the city and all of the once-elegant buildings, it was obvious that Tangier had belonged to the high-society in former times. Despite this, as made evident by the poverty that exists now, the city is known to be quite dangerous and you can actually feel this as you walk around. It was enjoyable to see such an interesting place, but at the same time, we didn't feel safe and were looking forward to moving on to somewhere else.

Getting into a conversation with our new-found friends from England, we started discussing the hygienic problem that still existed in the country, mentioning the fact that we had to get an array of shots before coming, including hepatitis, polio, diphtheria, tetanus, meningitis, and several others. Except for the malaria pills, which were only necessary if we intended to travel to the north of the country, the only thing we hadn't been injected for was rabies. We didn't want to spend the money for it and told ourselves that we would simply avoid contact with animals.

Unfortunately for us, later on during our vacation, a rabies warning for Morocco was issued by the Austrian government. During the week we were on our honeymoon, an Austrian traveler had died, having contracted rabies from a dog just east of where we were. This turned out to be a constant stress, especially considering the fact that there were stray dogs and cats in every direction we looked.

After doing a bit of sightseeing, we decided to get something to eat. When in a foreign country, it is always a good idea to pick out a restaurant where you see a lot of local inhabitants inside. You will be assured that the food is tasty, clean, and inexpensive. In my experience, even the cleanest-looking restaurant can be deceiving. If a restaurant is empty, there is usually a reason.

As we entered a restaurant full of Moroccans, to my amazement, someone started yelling, "Mike, Mike!" The coincidence was absolutely unbelievable! It just so happened that my friend from Salzburg, Mohammad, was in that very restaurant. Katharina was also shocked that I suddenly knew someone in the middle of Morocco that she just stood with her mouth wide open at a complete loss of words. Greeting Mohammad in Arabic, the English people accompanying us, turned white in the face. They were speechless.

Ahmed greeted me in the traditional Arab way by hugging me and giving me kisses on the cheeks, and introduced me to his father who was wearing a white robe and head covering. He explained to me that he was in Morocco visiting his family and had just arrived to Tangier. At that moment, two chickens arrived on a platter with a side of hummus, salad, and a bottle of Coca-Cola. He told us that the meal was on him and, after promising to meet soon in Salzburg, he bid us farewell. What a warm welcome. During our meal, I had a lot of explaining to do.

We finally got on the night train. It was a wagon with four bunk beds and one giant window. Although the train was quite old, it was impeccably clean. Unfortunately, I was only able to sleep for a few hours because the train was going so fast that it felt like it was going to derail.

As dawn broke around four, I kept looking out of the window. It was mesmerizing; desert, clay houses, donkeys, old shanties, everything that I had only seen in films up until that point.

During the course of the morning, everyone was eventually awoken by a man coming through and selling coffee. Right then, someone in the neighboring cabin started playing a lute. The whole train woke up and as people started talking to each other, we started hearing Arabic in every which direction. Hearing the music, the foreign language all around us, and drinking the strong coffee, it was obvious that we were not in Europe anymore. Arriving in Marrakesh, we took leave from the English couple and took a cab into the city. To my surprise, the hotels offered a spot to sleep on the terrace of their roof amongst many other backpackers.

Alongside the sleeping area, there was a little bar where we had tea while looking at a panorama of the whole city around us. As we stood there, the call for prayer from the many mosques reverberated through the entire city. "*Allah wakbar, Allah wakbar, haya salaa, hayaa salaa'* - God is great, God is great, come to pray…"

We watched as many hurried to the mosques to pray or just stopped walking, laid a prayer rug out in front of them in the middle of the street and prayed.

At midday, we visited a *suuq*, an Arabic market, which was like traveling back in time. It was gigantic and full of hundreds of people. There were many little stands and open-air shops that were run-down and packed with wares to the ceiling; it was unbelievable. The market was divided into various areas. In one area, it was possible to buy food, spices, tobacco and pipes, and in another, jewelry and clothing were available. There was so much stuff to buy all cluttered up in the shops, giving the impression that everyone was trying to sell the exact same items, and yet, there were thousands of people scurrying to buy everything.

It wasn't possible to just look around in peace; we were forced to deal with the masses of people talking to us. Everybody was begging us to have a look in their shops, being quite pushy in the process. Some people even came up and took us by the arm pleading to view their merchandise.

In the middle of all this chaos, there was a murmuring of voices everywhere while mopeds were driving right through the crowd of people. It was amazing that no accidents occurred. We were even witness to a group of people arguing and eventually started fighting. The whole atmosphere was intense but also incredibly exhilarating.

At night, we went to the "*Place Djemaa el-Fna.*" Located in the center of the city, it is a square full of the most interesting things in the world, coming forth like a scene taken from *Arabian Nights.* We were surrounded by snake charmers, fortune-tellers, a food bazaar, and acrobats. There was even a man selling human teeth.

Weaving in and out through the masses of people, there were motor scooters everywhere, making the whole ambiance quite chaotic. People on the street kept approaching us, either asking for money or wanting to know if we wanted to buy *Moroccan chocolate.* It was only later, reading our guide book that we found out that they were asking us if we wanted to buy hashish.

The atmosphere was absolutely alive with music; not just the sound of the snake charmers playing their flutes but also a group playing Moroccan tribal music. The rhythms filled us with energy and excitement as we walked around in circles. Going back to sleep that night on the roof of the hotel, looking up at the stars, I could still hear the music playing and the voices of the crowds in the distance.

Going to the market again the next day, I grew weary of people begging us for money and asking us to look into their stores. I just wanted to be left alone, but decided to do one more thing before going back to the hotel. I went to the snake charmer to take a picture. He was sitting there playing a flute in front of a black cobra with a second big green snake wrapped across his neck. Thinking that no one at home would believe me, I wanted to bring proof of what I had seen.

At this square, it is said that everyone has eyes behind their heads. Although the area is full of amazing things, it is not possible to take a single picture without a mob of people coming up to you, demanding money for the photo. The day before, when we tried taking pictures inconspicuously, a group of people suddenly appeared out of nowhere wanting us to pay.

Despite this, I still wanted to get a picture of the cobra charmer and was even willing to pay a price. Asking him how much money a picture would cost, he said, "'*Kama turiid*' - However much you want." Then he put the green snake he had around my neck and I knelt in front of the black cobra. As Katharina backed up and started taking a picture, a man attempted to snatch her camera.

While he was trying to rip it out of her hands, I still had this green snake on my neck and was afraid to move. I screamed in Arabic, "*'Tilka zowjati, Daha!!'*- That is my wife, leave her!!" Men nearby heard this and came to Katharina's rescue. Then, the man with the snake demanded fifty dirham from me, which was like five dollars. I thought this was robbery for a mere picture and refused to pay.

"If you don't pay me, I'll let the snake bite you," he said. Agreeing to pay, I pretended to grab my wallet. After the snake had been removed from my neck and I was a safe distance away from the cobra, I took twenty dirham out of my pocket, two dollars, and threw it at him and ran.

I was shaken up by what had just happened, but also really angry! Suddenly realizing that Katharina had disappeared, I went searching for her amongst the masses of people. After finally spotting her, it was evident that she was forcefully being held by a woman that was painting her arm with henna as she was screaming to get away.

She had tears in her eyes while she was yelling out, "NO, please stop!"

The lady gripping her was saying, "A present, I give you PRESENT!"

I ran to her, screaming like a madman at the lady, "What are you doing!!"

She let go of Katharina's arm and demanded, "Give me one hundred dollars!"

I was not ready to give her anything, especially considering that she had just forced her services upon my wife. Yet, there were some men behind us that had previously witnessed the scene I made with the snake charmer. They were looking at me with disapproval, which made me worry. Without a second thought, I pulled another twenty dirham out of my wallet and said, "'*Huz haza badl ukhabiru ashhurta!!*'—Take this or I'll call the police!" She grabbed what I offered and disappeared into the crowd of people. Collecting our thoughts, we both went back to the hotel shaking.

The next day, we decided not to call ourselves defeated and went back to the market to look around. In our minds, we wanted to prove that it hadn't had the best of us, and went to the food bazaar, which smelled incredible. Music was playing, lights were everywhere and the smell of all the grilled food was out of this world. Among the smoke coming from the *shish-kebab*, there was the smell of lamb, beef, and mutton. Unfortunately, the only thing we could eat was meat, couscous, and olives.

In Morocco, as a westerner, you couldn't drink the water without getting travel sickness (diarrhea and vomiting) and that meant you couldn't eat any fruits or vegetable that you cannot peel. My wife, who is only used to eating meat like three times a week or even less, was having quite a dilemma. Looking at the delicious salad and fresh fruit on her plate, she could not hold herself back and ate it all. "I am sure that the warning about the water is over-exaggerated," she said.

Having a mint tea afterwards, the national

drink of Morocco, and going back to the hotel, we tried to relax as we lay in our sleeping bags on the roof of the hotel, again looking at the stars. It was very difficult to fall asleep because of all the music being played at the market. At first, the excitement of staying at a hotel that was centrally located was very enthusing, but now we just needed rest. After finally falling asleep, we were awoken by the call of the mosques a few hours later. I wanted to go home already, and it was only our third day in Morocco.

The next morning, I was ready to leave Marrakesh, but there was one more thing that we had to see before leaving, the tannery. Finding our way there was very strenuous. A man we asked directions from insisted that he be paid to show us personally. After thankfully refusing his help, he decided not to give us a choice and pursued us for miles, demanding payment for his services. Having told the man in both Arabic and French that we knew the way and did not need him to accompany us, he started screaming. As far as he was concerned, he was the only one that knew the way to the tannery and his presence was mandatory.

Katharina and I were quite afraid of what was happening. It was an extremely odd situation, especially considering that this strange man seemed quite violent in nature. Even though we ignored him and tried to pick up our pace in order to outrun him, he continued his pursuit. I was full of adrenaline, partly out of fear and partly out of anger. Despite our pleas, he would not leave us alone.

Finally arriving at the gates of the tannery, we ran in and asked for a tour. The man following us tried to get in as well, but I told the tour guide that he was not with us and I explained the situation. He closed the gate, but the scary man stood waiting there for us to come out. In his mind, he had just taken us to our destination and wanted to receive his just earnings.

The tannery was really interesting. We learned about how leather goods were prepared in Morocco using the most ancient of methods known to mankind. They still use cow urine to prepare the leather, and then they soak the leather in a mixture of flour to take out the smell. The man gave us mint leaves to put up under our noses because the smell of the urine was unbearable. After the tour, dreading the man waiting for us outside, I paid the guide quite a large tip asking him if it would be possible to distract the scary man in order for us to leave in peace. Our guide went outside the gate and started yelling. I don't know what he said, but the man followed us no more. At that moment, we actually began to feel sorry for him, because he must have been very poor to be driven to do such a ludicrous act.

Essauira, the next city we visited in Morocco, was wonderful, peaceful, and all in all quite relaxing. The Doors, Jim Morrison, and Jimi Hendrix all had residencies there. In the seventies, it was a meeting place for hippies. In fact, we learned that a lot of the hippie fashion during the era actually originated from the Moroccan culture.

We found a restaurant that served alcoholic beverages in their attic. Alcohol is generally illegal in public places, as it is in many Islamic countries. Some restaurants have special permission, but the drinking area has to be separated from Muslim guests. After having a few drinks, we did something crazy and went to the beach to ride camels. Afterwards, while watching the sunset with Katharina, on the high walls of the city looking over the ocean I thought of how much I loved my wife. This was truly our honeymoon!

On our way to Casablanca, we had what we called 'the bus ride from hell'. The bus was hot, there was no music, and above all, it kept stopping. It smelled bad, like an armpit that had not seen deodorant for a long time. Suddenly, the bus stopped in the middle of a desert for about forty-five minutes. We thought it was broken down and we started getting really worried. The bus driver shockingly ordered all women to stay in the bus. Going outside to the big group of men talking, I saw the man who originally collected our bus tickets. He was about my age with black oil smeared all over his face wearing a tattered shirt.

"What is the matter? Has the bus broken down?" I asked.

"Give me a cigarette and I will tell you," he said. Thinking how strange his response was, I took one out of the package in my pocket and gave it to him.

"The bus is not broken down," he said lighting the cigarette, inhaling and then blowing a smoke ring, "No diesel."

We were in the middle of a desert with no fuel. While thinking of our demise, the first thing I did was to go to Katharina and tell her to hide the water. After explaining what the problem was, we just sat there with a 'this-is-unbelievable' look on our faces. I kept repeating that everything would be okay, although I was in a state of shock.

After a while, another bus came from the other direction and stopped. Then, out of nowhere, a donkey appeared carrying a wagon on it with tanks. I watched as a man sucked on a giant tube and spit out diesel from the other bus. It was then transferred by the tanks the donkey was carrying and put into our bus. It was enough fuel to get us to the next gas station. The driver paid the other bus driver the money for the gas and we were on our way.

As it turned out, my wife did get sick eating the salads. Staying at a very cheap hotel that only cost us four dollars a night, the room didn't have a bathroom except for a hole in the ground and its only window looked out on to a fish grill which made my wife even more ill. We spent most of the time in Casablanca in search of a normal toilette so my wife could vomit. Strangely enough, we found one at a local McDonald's. It was not until later that I accidentally ate an ice cube in one of my drinks causing me to get sick as well. Luckily, I had it much easier than my wife because I didn't have to search and already knew where the McDonald's was located.

The next day, we took the train to Fés. It was

so full of travelers that we had to stand for most of the trip. We ended up finding a place to sit in a compartment with four other people.

I started talking about religion, which in the Muslim world is a very lively topic. Finishing a sentence, I said, "'*Inshaa Allah'*- If it is God's will!" This is a very common interjection in the Arabic language and it requires a response.

Three of the four other people in compartment started chanting at the same time, "*Inshaa Allah! Inshaa Allah,*" quite loudly. The only person that did not say anything, except for my wife, was an Arab with a really long beard and very dark skin. I started talking with him when he suddenly said, "I don't speak Arabic, I am American. Do you speak English?"

He explained that he was a graduate from Harvard on a grant allowing him to travel to Morocco in order to learn French and Arabic. Amusingly enough, he explained that he wanted to dress like an Arab so he did not stick out so much and get bothered on the street. He was even wearing Moroccan garments, had a deep brown tan, and even grew his beard down to his waist. I thought about this for a while, but it all seemed to make such perfect sense that it scared me. "It's time we go home soon," I thought.

CHRISTMAS

I t was snowing outside and my wife and I were in a coffee house having a tremendous Austrian breakfast. It is much different to breakfast in the US, mainly consisting of tea or coffee, Kaiser rolls, jam, butter, ham, cheese, and a soft-boiled egg. As always, everything had been served on little silver trays at our cozy little table. The coffee house was already decorated for the Christmas season, smoke was lingering through the air, and people were reading newspapers while drinking their coffee.

Coffee in Austria is more than just a drink; it is an institution. Austria is known for all of its elegant coffee houses and its very special, very strong, thick and creamy coffee that has a tremendous history. It was originally brought by the Turks in 1683. Since then, it has even become a tradition to sit in a café with one cup of coffee and the many newspapers lying around, reading for hours or talking in a state of complete relaxation. In my opinion, ordering breakfast in an Austrian café, which on Sunday in addition to the meal, also consists of a glass of champagne and a cup of coffee, is one of the most enjoyable things that the country has to offer.

On this particular occasion, we were talking about how we would handle Christmas when we had children. The holiday season is celebrated much differently in Austria than in the United States. I started thinking of all the different, weird, and wonderful Christmas traditions in Austria.

That year, the Christmas markets had opened up early and we had already gone on a stroll through the big open market on the square in front of the cathedral. I always loved to smell the gingerbread, admire the thousands of different Christmas ornaments and drink a cup of *Glühwein*, hot red wine flavored with spices, out in the cold. It makes you stay warm while contemplating what to buy at the market and visiting with friends. Youngsters and adults alike meet at the markets for a *Glühwein* to enjoy the Christmas atmosphere. Amongst all of these people, I can usually be spotted every single year with a steaming mug and a red mustache from the wine on my lip.

The Christmas Market in Salzburg is over five-hundred years old. They have choirs singing and trumpets playing. It is pure Christmas in every sense of the word.

Considering the fact that all of this is so magical, I have always been stunned by another common tradition in the Alp region that never seemed to fit into the heavenly atmosphere of the Christmas season at all. It is a very old custom, actually going back to Pagan times and revealing the rough side of life in the Alps. I started avoiding the city on December 5. My wife, on the other hand, enjoyed taking me to the best places to watch a "*Krampuslauf*". That year, she had taken me to a small village outside of Salzburg. In the darkness, hundreds of people were waiting at the market square and along the main street. Suddenly, I could hear the sound of cow bells and the first people screaming down the road. The parade had just begun. As they were nearing us, I could smell the pungent odor of damp fur when the first of the *Krampus* suddenly appeared out the distance. The beast was dressed in long, black fur with huge cow bells tied to his back and a wooden mask with long animal horns on its head. In its hand, he was holding a cow tail and a long threatening switch made of wood. Although I knew it was just a young man in a costume, the horrible beast with its long teeth, big open mouth, and green evil eyes scared me to death. Down the road, I could see the carriage with Saint Nicolas being drawn by two of the *Krampuses,* surrounded by more of these devilish creatures parading around on floats full of open fire. I could hear the drums beating and the sound of hellish cow bells ringing. In the mean time there was quite a bit of movement going on as people tried to escape getting beaten. Originally a Pagan tradition to chase away winter, the *Krampus* now accompanies Saint Nicolas, a saint who traditionally brings gifts for the children on December 6, and actually inspired the myth of our Santa Claus. The *Krampus* is a symbol for evil or for the devil and is cast away by Saint Nicolas. Only the bad children have to fear his switch or be afraid of having coal instead of sweets in their gift bags.

My nieces and nephews never have coal in their bags. That year a man came to Katharina's sister's house, dressed as St. Nicolas, in red canonical robes with a long white beard, carrying a scepter and bearing gifts for the children. Even though there was no *Krampus* in sight, the children deeply revered the bishop and were on their best behavior while the adults were feasting upon roasted chestnuts and punch.

Sipping on my coffee and talking to Katharina about all of these strange traditions, I mentioned my first Christmas in Austria and how I spent it with an old girlfriend and her family years before. I remember the beautiful Christmas Eve party at her house with gifts being exchanged, Christmas carols, and a nice fish dinner. How incredibly disappointing it was on the following day when I woke up, only to find out that there was no celebration on December 25. When I asked my girlfriend, who was reading a book, when we would finally celebrate Christmas and eat turkey, she looked at me with surprise and said: "We already celebrated Christmas. It was yesterday!" I was horrified and felt as if I had missed Christmas.

I learned that in Austria, Christmas was called "*Weihnachten*" (literally "holy night") and celebrated at night on Christmas Eve. December 25, was considered a day to relax and spend with the family.

Since then, I have become used to celebrating on Christmas Eve and I even look forward to my mother-in-law's traditional mayonnaise salad and fish. As evening falls, we have dinner, sing Christmas songs and eat cookies! My mother-in-law usually bakes about fifteen different kinds during the holiday season. The children are bouncing off the walls and aren't allowed to go into the living room until they hear the bell of an angel. The Christ Child, who is invisible, brings the decorated tree and the gifts. Therefore, the door of the living room stays closed the entire day on Christmas Eve. In reality, my in-laws usually spend the whole night before putting up the tree and decorating it. To me, this has always seemed quite stressful.

Discussing all of this in detail with my wife was of utmost importance. This topic will be a deciding factor of how we raise our children and how we handle Christmas for them in the future. Should we do it the American way or the Austrian way?

Personally, I like having a tree up during the Christmas season. Yet, when our children start school, it would be pretty confusing if they were told that the Christ Child brings the tree on Christmas Eve, especially if it is already decorated and in our living room.

After the bell finally rings, the children go into the living room to see what the Christ Child has brought for them. They are full of immense happiness when they see the tree, all lit with candles and presents lying under it. The children are not allowed to go to the presents until the traditional song has been song. It is not common that the song is played in any public place in Salzburg until Christmas Eve when the Christ Child comes to bring the presents, namely the song *Stille Nacht.* This song is better known in English as *"*Silent Night*"*.

"Silent Night" is such a popular song; I was quite surprised when I found out that it originated in Austria and that its original version is actually German. Legend has it that on December 24, 1818, there was a problem with the church's organ in the small village of Oberndorf, just outside of the city of Salzburg. In desperation to have music for the Christmas mass, Father Mohr gave a poem he had written two years earlier to Franz Gruber and asked him to write something. "Silent Night" was performed on that Christmas Eve in the St. Nicolas Church and practically saved the holiday. The song had been written for soprano, tenor, choir, and guitar.

"Silent Night" remains to this very day a very special and sacred song in Salzburg and its surroundings. In contrast to many cities around the world where the song is played throughout the entire season, it can only be heard in Salzburg on Christmas Eve, and is very reluctantly listened to beforehand.

After the magical moment of the family choir, the children are allowed to open their presents. At this moment, a bottle of champagne is opened and a toast is made to one another, walking around to each member of the family, looking into each other's eyes, clinging the glasses together, saying "Merry Christmas", shaking hands, then giving a hug and kiss. It is quite magical.

On Christmas Day, Katharina and I have started to celebrate a little bit of "American" Christmas for me. For the last five years, I have introduced "American" Christmas traditions, on December 25, to my Austrian family. In the beginning, they were skeptical, but they now actually look forward to my turkey dinner. A few years ago, my mother sent us gifts for my nieces and nephews. On each package was written: "From Santa". We gave them to the kids saying it was from an American gift-giver named Santa Claus, who came all the way from the USA for Uncle Michael and the rest of his family. Every year, they still ask if Santa is going to come to them again. If I ever get accused of Americanizing an Austrian family, I'll have to admit I have.

After talking for a while and having our breakfast, we came to the conclusion that our children will be just about the luckiest children on Earth. They are going to have all that Austria has to offer as well as Santa Claus, even though they may be taught that Santa comes from the United States instead of the North Pole, but that hasn't been decided yet.

CROSSING BORDERS

C rossing the border in Europe or anywhere else in the world means a lot more than just crossing into another territory, it means going into another world, being faced with another reality. There are different laws and a different language which govern the land, not to mention the different history of each nation. Therefore, the mentality and way of thinking that people have change. Along with the differences concerning the standard of living, the whole idea of how a person should live changes. This can often be quite irrational for the foreign visitor.

With the type of world we have today, where it is possible to travel across the Earth in a single afternoon and talk with a person located miles away for virtually nothing, much less send them a picture or a video, it is hard to believe that we are so different. Yet, it is necessary to think that this has actually taken place over the last twenty years. Twenty years ago, it was not so self-explanatory for a person to simply fly to their destination. If you traveled to Europe from the United States, you were considered a world traveler. Now, if you fly to Paris over the weekend, you've just had a crazy weekend in Europe. It always astonishes me how much life, travel, and communication have sped up. Yet, the differences still exist and can be easily discovered, especially in Europe where everything is so close together and, at the same time, far apart.

When my two older sisters came to visit me in my first year in Austria, they were simply amazed that they could visit so many different countries in a short period of time. Austria borders eight different countries: Italy, Switzerland, Lichtenstein, Germany, the Czech Republic, Slovakia, Hungary, and Slovenia. On account of the fact that Austria is such a small nation, it is possible to reach these countries by car or train within a day, a few hours or in some cases, a few minutes. Although the countries are all very close, where you cross makes a world of difference. Austria has always been known as the gateway to Eastern Europe.

In 2000, crossing from Austria into the Czech Republic, in Eastern Europe, was like going to another world. If you live in the northern parts of Austria, it is just a short drive away. There was an incredible gap between the two countries with regard to the standard of living. Crossing the border, it was evident that even the smell of the air changed on account of the fact that car emissions were not regulated. It was amazing to see that just by crossing a fictional line and going through a checkpoint, there would be so many differences. Suddenly, the cars were much older and the buildings were run down and were all together much smaller.

While crossing the border itself, you had to get your passports checked and it was not completely free of risk. If you arose any type of suspicion, they had the right to keep you for hours, check your car, and go through your luggage. During the times of communism, it was almost impossible to enter the country and there have even been cases of people getting their tires shot out or not being allowed entry.

When the iron curtain fell, the Austrians actually had to get used to the fact that they were able to enter their neighboring country. Since the Czech Republic joined the European Union, it feels strange that you don't even need to show a passport when crossing from one country's border into another.

Right behind the border, there were several prostitutes running at cars, some of them quite young. Most of the Austrian and German towns near the border have trouble with the high rate of AIDS because of this. I was once invited to a friend's house in Germany. His town was located about fifteen minutes from the border of the Czech Republic. In all the pubs at night, there were activists handing out condoms and information about safe sex.

When entering Eastern Europe, there were always intense differences. Now, with the European Union, the differences are still there, but are not as evident as they once were. A lot of problems, as well as the poverty that communism caused, has not been gotten rid of, but there is a sign that things are getting better. Last year I went to Poland driving through the Czech Republic and was simply amazed how much had changed since my first visit to the country. Houses were being renovated and all around you could see big international chains being opened. Just some years before, the air of the communist era could still be felt. Now, the outskirts of the cities with their huge shopping malls have started to look just the same as anywhere else in the western world.

MOVING SOUTH

F inally arriving at our destination, after having traveled for so many hours throughout the night and a good portion of the day, I looked around and saw all of the palm trees and run-down buildings, smelling a sweet saltiness with a light touch of car exhaust in the air. Having just driven through Rome, which is known for its chaotic traffic, we were expecting our arrival to be relatively relaxing. On the contrary; gazing from the passenger seat, I noticed hundreds of cars, weaving in and out, going through stoplights, and honking their horns. One single thought was running through my mind again and again; this was going to be our new home.

Walking into the apartment with its stone floors, it reminded me very much of Egypt and Morocco. The sun shone through the large windows and the whole atmosphere had quite a raw beauty to it. Aside from this, it was really dirty and I knew we had a lot of work ahead of us. To our dismay, we found out that the apartment did not have any electricity or water in it.

We called our landlord to tell him about our trouble. He came to meet us right away. After kissing both me and my wife on the cheeks to greet us, he told us not to worry about the electricity or the water. "It is just a matter of a phone call," he said. Only later did we find out that technicians had to come to turn on the basic necessities in our apartment and we were going to have to survive for two weeks without any water or electricity until they came. "This is the south of Italy," we thought.

Waking up in the morning to the sounds of motor scooters driving up and down the streets and people yelling everywhere, we decided to go out and have a look at our new neighborhood. Going down our street situated in the ancient city, we noticed several old buildings and many people walking out of cave-like houses on the ground floor, all wearing pajamas. In addition, there were a lot of little shops selling food. There was even a butcher on the corner that would stock up his shop every morning with a rack of meat over his shoulder. The honking of car horns intertwined with the many other noises under the hot sun and the salty-smelling air. I was in Bari, Italy, the beginning of a completely new chapter in my life.

Two months later, we finally got our apartment in order. It took us quite a while to get used to the neighbors and for them to get accustomed to us. Our landlord warned us that we had to treat them with respect but not get too friendly or close because they could cause us problems. In fact, many of them had just taken over empty apartments and were living there illegally. Every time we passed them when leaving our apartment building, they were grilling on the street or eating. We said, "*Buongiorno*" and they retorted with either a mean sort of grimace or just completely ignored us altogether. For them, our presence was like having a visit from another planet. We were foreigners or as you would say in Italian, '*gli stranieri*'.

From our apartment, it was about a three-minute walk to the seaside on foot. At first, we thought this was great. After all, Bari is the sunniest place in all of Italy with an average of about three hundred days of sunlight per year. What better place to live than right near the sea. Then we found out that due to the moisture, there were thousands of mosquitoes that visited our apartment every evening throughout the year, causing us to have to buy a mosquito net for the bed. It was horrifying because they were absolutely enormous and were so fast that I could not even kill them. Even after closing the mosquito net, it was not possible to keep every single one out. I will never forget those little vampire insects.

One day, after going for a walk at the seaside, we decide to go to my favorite coffee shop at the city square called the Piazza Ferrarese. Sitting down, the waitress came immediately. She always greeted me with a smile saying, "*Ciao*, Michael!" kissing both of my cheeks and completely ignoring my wife. It was for this reason that Katharina absolutely hated going to this coffee house.

Having an Italian cappuccino and sitting in the sun were the best moments of my life. Despite the constant uneasiness caused by the confrontation between my wife and the waitress, it was still my absolute favorite place to drink coffee and have a chocolate croissant to start the morning. Drinking coffee in the sunlight, looking out into the sea with its many ships, smelling the salty air, I was in heaven. Getting ready to leave the café, we tried to get the waitresses attention so that we could pay for our coffee and croissants. The waitress signaled to us that she had to smoke her cigarette. It took another half hour before we were able to pay the bill.

As we walked back into our neighborhood with its narrow streets and tall buildings, we were greeted by the butcher and Nino, the local mini-market owner. Nino, a robust Italian man with a big nose and glasses, sold all types of wine, salami and cheeses which tasted so good that they just melted in your mouth. He was also an expert on food and could always recommend something in his shop that sold at sky-rocket prices.

Just then, he approached us asking why we hadn't been going to his shop for a while. We apologized and said that, although his food was good, we just couldn't afford it. A pint of milk, a bottle of oil and a can of tomatoes cost over twelve euros. He must have understood how we felt because he started lowering his prices as time went by. Eventually, his shop became even cheaper than our local supermarket.

The butcher across from Nino's shop was incredibly nice to us. In fact, he was the friendliest person in our whole neighborhood, always greeting us with a smile. Talking with my wife one day, I said, "It is a pity that we do not buy more meat from the butcher's on the corner. The hamburgers we got there once were so good."

My wife said, "Yes, but the last time we were there, he said he only had horse meat that day. And you know how much I love horses." In the South of Italy, horse meat is quite a delicacy. Because the butcher was so small, sometimes he only had a few things to choose from. Since the day he only had '*equino*', she had never gone back again. After pleading with her, we finally ended up going to him again.

"What type of meat do you have today?" asked my wife.

"*Equino*," he said quite naturally.

"Well, the thing is, my wife and I would like to start buying more from your shop. Unfortunately, my wife doesn't like horse meat. In Austria, she rides horses and doesn't like to eat them."

"I only sell horse meat. I am a horse butcher," he said as Katharina's face revealed her thoughts of eating the hamburgers we had had once before.

"I thought those hamburgers tasted funny," she said with a red face.

That day was the October 31, and our first Halloween in Italy. Halloween is actually an American holiday that has been brought over to Europe by television and global marketing. In Austria, for example, although a lot of kids dress up and go trick or treating, there are still people that forbid its celebrations due to the fact that it has nothing to do with Austrian tradition. In southern Italy, on the other hand, only about five percent of the population actually attempts to even celebrate the foreign holiday.

Looking down from our balcony at the street below us with a glass of red wine in my hand, I saw a bunch of little kids running through the streets screaming with empty pillowcases in their hands. They were not in disguises and didn't go door to door. They asked people walking along the street if they had any candy. If they were lucky, an old man passing would give them a piece of gum. This made me feel really sorry for them. Above all, I was so disappointed that I had bought a big bag of candy for nothing, thinking that the children might have come to our door.

Seeing that I still wanted to celebrate, I decided to take things into my own hands. I dressed up as a monster by gluing a napkin onto my face and ripping it up. I also borrowed some makeup from my wife and I have to say, after putting a throw rug over my shoulders, I really did look gruesome. I put the bag of caramel candy that I bought into a bowl and went downstairs. While doing so, my wife thought that I was completely insane and said, "I wouldn't do that. You know that our neighborhood is not the best and after all, our landlord said it would be better to keep a distance from the neighbors."

"They are just kids," I said and went downstairs to give out the candy. Opening the door to our apartment building and walking out onto our street, everyone looked at me and actually took cover trying to hide as if I was going to do them harm. Then I started yelling that I had candy for them, "*Dolcetti! Ho dolcetti per voi!*"

Suddenly, about ten kids started almost attacking the bowl of candy, screaming while gripping their hands into the bowl with such force that I thought I was going to fall over. They were trying to get as much as possible. In these few moments, I felt as if I was being mugged. The children, curious about my costume, started picking at the mask with their hands, scratching my face in the process while others were tackling me and the bowl of candy. In about thirty seconds, the whole bowl was empty and my costume was ruined. Suddenly, I noticed a huge mass of other children running toward me with their empty pillow sacks. They ALL wanted candy and I didn't have a single one left. Struggling, I was able to make it back into my door, trying not to hurt any of their hands as I closed it. After going upstairs to Katharina, shaken with my face all scratched and my costume all ruined, she said, "I told you that you shouldn't have done that."

That night, we had to listen to our doorbell ring for about an hour constantly. "I should have bought more candy," I thought as I fell asleep that night.

MY DREAMS AND INSPIRATION AND HOW IT ALL BEGAN

I never really had many ambitions to travel growing up. My mother had always taught me to be content with what I had, but she filled my mind full of fantasy, talking about the pyramids of Egypt and how amazing they were. My mother and father had once traveled to North Africa, the one huge trip that they had made in their lives. My father was a Vietnam veteran, so I guess Egypt was not his only trip oversees, but of the two, Egypt was the only one he cared to talk about.

They used to talk about how amazing it was. My mother, who was known to exaggerate quite a bit, filled my mind with all sorts of ideas. And not just about her trip to North Africa, she also read quite a bit and showed me and my sisters pictures of the Colosseum in Rome and talked about traveling the world as if she had been there herself. I think she placed a secret desire to travel in me and every single one of my three sisters.

I could not talk more vividly about my early aspirations to see the world without mentioning my grandmother, Kamoa, for she has been and always will be a huge inspiration in my life to do many things and to truly enjoy life. The name sounds a bit strange, doesn't it? Grandmother Kamoa is half Hawaiian and half American Indian. A hula-dancer by trade, she had traveled throughout the entire United States with the Ray Kinney Orchestra, a famous band in the fifties.

She has always been an interesting person, full of a million stories about herself, about others, but the thing I remember about my grandmother was her ability to talk to people and make them feel good about themselves. On account of this, she had always had a million friends. No one could spend five minutes talking with her without being immersed in a three hour conversation and afterwards, being filled with a great feeling of inner peace. This aspect of her always made me think that she was a type of angel.

My grandmother had another aspect about her that I think has contributed greatly to my way of thinking, right to this very day. She has always considered herself, and I quote, "A woman of the world." She had a never-ending ability to accept people, no matter what their color, age, race, or nationality. Above all, she absolutely loved culture. It was not until my early twenties that I finally realized how many friends she had from Germany, the Middle East, India, and the Orient. Even my grandfather had Italian roots, which always caused my grandmother to share her views about his family and the old world. All this had a huge impact upon my life.

Music actually brought me to leave the United States. I worked for a long time in my father's music shop as a salesman. My father's music shop had mainly been a rock store that sold guitars and other music supplies. Although I played trumpet in my high school band, I always wanted to play a popular instrument like the guitar, but my father who had played professionally all of his life, never wanted me to become a musician. I guess he thought that I would have a better future if I kept away from it. For this reason, I started learning the guitar on my own.

After learning my very first song and being able to change between chords, I felt I was ready to go to a local café to sing and play at an open-mic night. This turned into a complete disaster, for I was the youngest person there in the midst of people that had been playing for several decades. Embarrassingly enough, the day of my first grand performance, a string broke. - With the will to become better, I started lessons with a rock guitarist. Having been a fan of guitar technique, he told me to buy a copy of *Eliot Fisk's Twenty-Four Capricci* by Nicolo Paganini. According to him, it was an example of the best technique ever. Putting in the disk and hitting play was the very first time that I had ever listened to classical guitar, it being the most beautiful thing I had ever heard. From that point on, it had been my desire to play that type of music.

Therefore, I called a local college, only to discover that I was too young to attend courses. In desperation, I called the guitar teacher at another university. Due to my determination, he taught me personally. That is when I met Sam, my first classical guitar teacher, whom I consider to have been one of the best I've ever had. Teaching me not only to play, he taught me to love the instrument, which in my opinion constitutes one of the hardest challenges for any teacher. Practicing several hours a day, I improved at a great rate and truly loved playing the guitar.

Just about to graduate from high school, it was my intention to study locally. Samuel, on the other hand, suggested going to the Academy for Music and Applied Art in Vienna, having been a student there himself. He told me that living and studying in another country would broaden my horizons, learning not only music but also another language and culture. But, due to my family's financial situation, this seemed completely out of reach. My mother and father did not see how it would be possible for me to just go abroad and were very angry at Sam for putting such crazy ideas into my head.

Samuel made it all happen, assuring me that studying in Europe was possible. To prepare, I started taking a beginning music theory class, a German class, and played a solo concert. In my concert program, I had written that it was my wish to study with Sam's former teacher in Vienna, Austria. I was seventeen years old and everything was falling into place.

I started a big countdown a year before going for the tryout. I was counting down the days until Vienna a year before I actually went. I read books and prepared and was more excited than I think anybody on Earth about the whole thing.

Vienna, Austria, home to great composers and musical masterminds, and there I was amidst this great city in June of 1995, not even knowing how to get from the airport to the city. I was eighteen years old.

On the day of the exam, it occurred to me how completely ignorant I was to guitar exams in general, much less in a foreign country. Entering the stage through a back door, I wanted to greet all the professors staring at me. Therefore, I got off the stage and shook their hands, introducing myself and trying to make a good impression. This had been quite a surprise to the judges. Realizing my mistake, I will never forget how the person whom I was trying to impress just sat looking at me with disapproval. For an Austrian, what I had unintentionally done was just plain rude.

I got onto the stage again and waited in anticipation until I was told to play. After only two bars of playing, I was told to stop. The judge had just looked at the concert program I had played in America and misunderstood my English, assuming I had written on it that I could undoubtedly study under him, whereby I had only expressed that it was my mere wish. I came to my own rescue and corrected him. Instead of this helping the matter, he asked me to leave. This was the most disappointing day of my whole life. In fact, it had almost been the end of my dreams.

In despair, having spent the day in the Prater where I won that huge teddy bear, I went back to where I was staying and met a woman who worked there. While she spoke to me in German, it was in that very moment that I can attest the proof of God's existence. For some strange reason, although my German was very poor, I understood everything she said as if it had been English. She told me that there were other schools. In my broken German, I expressed that I would be willing to do anything, just not go home a failure. She called the Mozarteum Academy for Music in Salzburg and signed me up for the following entrance exam in October, giving me hope.

I will never forget arriving back to the US and looking into my father's eyes, which were full of discontent. He almost fell back in his chair when I told him my plans of returning to Austria. I found out later how proud he was that I had the courage to make such a decision.

At the exam in Salzburg I played my heart out. The judges asked if I wanted to study with 'Eliot'. Due to his absence, I would have had to play for him again to be considered. From the indisputable voice coming from the committee, I knew they had not only accepted me, but were faced with the question of who would be my teacher. My intuition told me to seize the chance and I left the choice up to them. I only found out afterwards that they were talking about Eliot Fisk, the reason I had started playing guitar.

I started my studies with a famous Argentinean classical guitarist, Maria Isabell Siewers de Pazur. Although very knowledgeable, her teaching methods were not right for me. I learned a lot from her, yet somehow we never connected. I ended up breaking off my studies after only one year. It was just too much pressure; learning a new language, being away from home, studying the hardest I could.

After a short time, I made the decision to continue with the intention of changing teachers. I called Eliot Fisk and he briskly said that he had no room for me in his classes. Afterwards, I must have coincidentally run into Eliot in the city at least four times, impressing upon him not to say no to me without at least hearing me.

I will never forget what he said after playing for him for the first time. He told me, "Michael, you have absolutely no technique, but you play with so much feeling that ten percent of your playing is absolutely beautiful." For several years after that, he proved not only to be a great teacher, but very good friend.

Eliot's promise to make me a guitarist became a reality. Samuel, my very first guitar teacher, made the trip to Austria to be there at my final concert and see me get my master's degree. He was right there with me when he said that studying abroad would broaden my horizons. In fact, it even made my dreams come true.

There are still new experiences, new challenges that I am confronted with. After spending two years in the south of Italy, my wife and I ended up settling down in a city I would have never expected to live in. We now live in Vienna. We actually don't live that far from the Prater. I am able to look out of the window and see that gigantic Ferris wheel I had been so excited about seeing during my very first week in Austria.

Printed in the United States
220009BV00005B/2/P